D1484197

LEVEL JUMPING

How I grew my business to over

$1 million in profits in 12 months

by Mike Simmons

ISBN: 978-1-7348327-0-9

This book is dedicated to the people who love and support me more than anyone.

My wife Nanette; the one who keeps me centered. The strongest, smartest, most understanding person I know.

My kids, Andrea, Lindsay and Blake. The absolute reason I work so hard to create things - to make them proud.

Finally, to those people in my life who have shown me a better, smarter way to get things done. I owe a lot of my success in business to their generosity and guidance.

CONTENTS

Introduction

Want a brain teaser? Some fun "mind candy" to expand your thinking?

Then try this.

Imagine you have a car and need to steer it. The catch is that the car is parked, and you're not allowed to turn it on.

How then do you steer this parked car?

Now, before you answer that, you'll probably want to do a Google search. Or maybe you'd rather check out some awesome productivity and life hack websites, especially if you already have a few bookmarked on your computer. Check those sites and see if anyone has posted advice. Or better yet, see if someone created an app to solve this problem.

Don't forget about podcasts and YouTube videos. With thousands upon thousands of them out there, chances are someone has said something useful, some unique insight you can use to crush this. Turn this piece of mind candy from jawbreaker to peanut butter cup.

Need a minute? You know, to search on Google. To check out productivity and life hack websites. To listen to podcasts. To watch YouTube videos.

Actually, that sounds silly, doesn't it? Because you'll probably need a whole lot longer than a minute. A few hours or even a few days is a better bet. But you're working full time, aren't you? And you may also have a spouse and kids.

So how about a month or even a few months? Does that work for you?

Maybe. But what if that's still not enough time? What happens if you need even longer to do all the necessary research and carefully consider how to move forward?

Well, then you might never solve this one. In fact, from the sound of things, you'd probably never even start working on solving it.

The parked car will remain exactly where it was: unmoved, despite your desire to steer it.

What's the point of all this? In other words, why am I giving you an abstract brainteaser to solve?

Relax. There's indeed a point, a method to my madness. And it's very relevant to you.

To see the connection, think back to what the original instructions were. There was a parked car and you had to steer it without turning the car on.

The big question, though, was how?

And the answer?

You don't.

Not without first turning the car on. Start the car so you can then steer it.

This solution probably seems obvious to you now. Stupid even, considering how simplistic it is. Yet look how complicated we made the situation, how we added layer after layer of research and preparation. To an extent, that eventually became overwhelming. And by the end, you probably didn't remember what we were talking about in the first place.

There's a lesson here, one that's as obvious as the answer to the brainteaser.

It's also a painful lesson, something that can cut to the core of your own identity, slicing it apart like the shredder at a deli counter.

What's the lesson?

Hold that thought. Before we get to it, let's talk about you. That way, you'll have a better context for understanding just how painful this lesson can be.

Consider who you are.

Obviously, you're special, a unique snowflake as so many motivational people like to say.

I hate to break any delusions you may have of being special, but actually, those delusions have probably already been broken. Especially today, given the rise of anti-motivators, guys from the motivational track who've changed their tune from feel-good fluff to tough love.

But I digress.

Back to you. We can safely assume you're interested in starting your own business or scaling an existing one. That desire is what led you to pick up this book in the first place.

That desire has also, in all likelihood, led you to educate yourself about business and entrepreneurship. This would explain the other content you've consumed so far, all of those other books, and perhaps podcasts, blog articles, YouTube videos, and much more.

It's an overwhelming amount, to be sure. But this kind of overwhelm is the fun type, where it's enjoyable to have so much content available, especially given that it all *seems* worthwhile in educating yourself, preparing you for the big day when you'll either open your business or embark on new efforts to scale the current one.

The question, though, is how much content do you need? How much is enough before you're properly armed for combat in the arena called business?

Right now, if you're paying attention, you may see where this is going. So, let's not beat around the proverbial bush. Time for the big reveal as they call it on those makeover TV shows.

The big reveal is that you have enough content already, enough that you can at least, at the very least, just start. Take that first step. The one that's supposedly how a journey of a thousand miles begins.

Will you travel that far? Maybe, maybe not. Yet you can still start.

But that's easier said than done, particularly given how attached you may be to consuming content and to the identity of aspiring entrepreneur.

Actually, you're more like an uninspiring Wantra-Preneur.

Ouch!

That was kind of a low blow. Hurts too, doesn't it?

Sure, but you were warned earlier, when we talked about the painful lesson to be learned and how it could slice to the core of your identity.

Talking about the pain means we've now come full circle, back to where we began with that brainteaser, the one about steering the parked car.

Connect the dots and you'll see a parallel to starting/scaling a business. In both cases, there's a tendency to go on a knowledge and content binge. Such a binge, in fact, that we never take that first step, whether the step relates to business or turning the key in the car's ignition.

The bottom line is that you just need to start doing what *you* can, where *you* are, with what *you* have.

You, you, you. But what about me?

Seriously, who the hell am I, the author, to be lecturing at you like this? To smugly call you an uninspiring Wantra-Preneur and insist that all you need is to just start? What gives me the right to engage in all this grandstanding?

So what am I? Or, rather, who the hell am I?

The short answer is, I don't know.

I don't know in the sense that I don't know what you're specifically looking to know, what magic details about my background will instantly put you at ease in reading this book.

I'm not going to dodge your question, though, since you've got every right to ask it. So let me give you the long answer.

The long answer is that I'm arguably the last person you'd ever expect to start a business. Yet today I own and operate, or am a partner in, multiple, million-dollar businesses.

What happened?

Let's rewind and see.

Go back to my early life and you'll find that I definitely did not live in an entrepreneurial ecosystem. In place of, say, Silicon Valley, I grew up in Michigan. So no, I wasn't exactly surrounded by entrepreneurs growing up. Nothing that would predispose me to start my own business. In fact, as a child, I was actively discouraged from doing anything entrepreneurial.

The ones advising me against it were my parents. Both my biological father and my stepfather (my parents divorced when I was two) worked in the automotive industry their whole lives. We lived in Michigan, a state where the automotive industry is a huge influence. As a result, union thinking, not entrepreneurialism, was the view held by those in my family.

In place of the unconventional entrepreneurial path, my parents encouraged me to pursue a conventional formula. Their formula went something like this:

1. Go to school.

2. Work for a union-backed company.

3. Earn a stable paycheck from the company, along with benefits (medical, dental, etc.).

4. Plant your roots at that one company, no changing jobs.

5. Work every opportunity you get — weekends, holidays, overtime, etc.

6. Repeat step 5 for 30+ years, and then eventually retire.

Sounds good, doesn't it? I certainly thought so. Part of it, of course, was that I respected my parents — and still do! So when they repeatedly advised me on the way it was for those in the working world, I readily agreed. After all, they were my parents.

Besides, I didn't even know there was another way. Being an entrepreneur just wasn't on the menu, so to speak. It's like eating hamburgers your whole life and never realizing that there are other foods out there, like lobster, pasta, or curry. A classic case of not knowing what you don't know.

What I did know, however, was to follow the formula, those six steps my parents had drilled into me at various stages while growing up.

Predictably, I went to college, though not right out of high school, and found a good stable employer. I was, however, a little rebellious in choosing my employer.

The rebellious element? My employer wasn't a union company. Radical, huh?

Maybe...until you consider that the company I joined was also in the auto industry. So the apple, as they say, didn't fall too far from the tree. Barring the union part, my employment and career were nearly identical to what my parents' had been.

And you know what? I was content. I spent my days working for the man in a stable corporate J.O.B. Back then, my goal was to work my way up the proverbial ladder.

Hopefully you see now why I'm undoubtedly the person least likely to become an entrepreneur. It's just not something I had any exposure to or knowledge of while growing up. It's also completely contrary to my parents' advice.

Given that background, where I am now, with multiple, highly profitable businesses, is therefore the ultimate 180. It's a shift about as far in the opposite direction as humanly possible.

If I can make that shift, can't you?

I believe you can. Some of you probably don't need to make as much of a shift as I did, especially if you're already reading a book like this.

I didn't have a book. What I did have, however, was anxiety about my retirement. That ended up being a major driver for me in starting the first of my businesses, back in the day.

Perhaps you've gone, as I did, and calculated the amount of money you'll need for retirement. If you haven't, I strongly recommend doing so. It'll be eye-opening for you, just as it was for me.

In my case, I remember running the numbers and realizing I couldn't retire at age 50 or 60. Not at the pace I was moving in the corporate world. At that pace, I would have to put off retirement until I reached at the ripe old age of 130.

Not 13. Not 30. 130 years old.

I don't know about you, but I definitely won't live to see 130 or anything close. So if the age I calculated for retirement was 130, the reality is that I would never be able to retire. Instead, I'd have to work steadily until the day I figuratively punched out of life.

This knowledge chilled me to the bone. As loyal as I was to my employer and the establishment, I was still a regular guy. And like most regular guys, I didn't want to just work. There were plenty of other things I'd rather do than work all day every day for my employer. Travel was one of those other things, as was spending more time with my family.

If you're like most people, you can probably relate to my dilemma. Chances are you want more time for pursuits outside of work. How, though, do you go about getting that extra time?

How? You do it in the same way I did. You take matters into your own hands by starting your own business.

In my case, the business was real estate investment (REI). Of all the possible fields, I chose REI because real estate had always interested me. My interest wasn't necessarily a passion, but I did find the material intriguing.

Driven by this interest and a desire to retire in this lifetime, I launched my own business.

Actually, that's not quite true. I mean, I did eventually launch my own business. But the road to reaching that point was littered with stumbles and falls. Moreover, I wrestled with the very same opponent you've faced, this opponent being the paralyzing feeling of not knowing enough to begin.

Fortunately, I faced this opponent back in the Dark Ages. The Dark Ages, of course, were those times when, believe it or not, people actually lived without social media, podcasts, and YouTube. Those things had yet to become fixtures in our daily lives.

The benefit of starting my own business in those Dark Ages was that the volume of existing entrepreneurial content was nowhere near what it is today. The amount of content back then was akin to a low-pressure kitchen faucet, not the fire hose of information we drink from today.

Of the entrepreneurial content that did exist in those days, books were the most prevalent. So when I decided to start my own business — in REI — I felt the need to read or at least to skim books. Because logically, it seemed like a mistake to just dive into business. I wanted to carefully learn everything that was needed before starting. Otherwise I could make a mistake.

Laughable, isn't it, that fear of making a mistake? As though a business could possibly be launched with no mistakes and 100% smooth sailing.

News flash: it can't. Mistakes will be made. They come with the territory when starting a business, as they do with any major undertaking in life. Deep down, I knew that, like you probably do. Yet we often turn a blind eye to that reality, pretending that it's indeed possible to begin in business without any bumps in the road.

What we need then, you and I, is the confidence to ignore that voice inside that doesn't us want to start yet. It's the same voice that believes we need to consume a perpetual diet of entrepreneurial/business content before we can launch our ventures.

This voice, though, is ultimately a sniveling coward. It's not really interested in learning more. No, learning, education, and careful preparation are really just disguises for fear, fear of the unknown, with the unknown in this case being what it's like to actually start and run a business.

Make no mistake: education is important. You probably don't want, for example, a chiropractor cracking your back without having been properly educated. Nor would you want a roofing company tearing up your roof without training on how to put on a new one correctly.

Nevertheless, education can also be comparable to quicksand, trapping aspiring entrepreneurs. The trap comes because education is safe. Sure, you can go into debt from some education, especially at the university level. But otherwise, education is basically risk-free.

After all, what's the worst that can happen if you watch a YouTube video or listen to a podcast episode on starting your own business?

Is there any risk?

Anything?

Nope. Not unless you're driving while watching the YouTube video and aren't looking at the road.

So you don't see that eighteen-wheeler truck until...

...you get the idea.

Other than that, there's no risk to education.

The goal of education, though, is to prepare you for execution. Eventually, for example, chiropractors graduate from their training programs and open their practices. So too with roofers. Once their apprenticeships end, it's time for them to begin actually installing roofs.

Execution, however, is fraught with risk. Losing money is one such risk and there are plenty of others specific to your particular industry or field.

When such risks evolve into actual problems, you'll need to correct your course. Steer as needed in order to resolve the situation.

Steering? Yes, as in steering a car. Which, as you know by now, can't be done when the car is parked.

The car needs to have its ignition flipped on and be moving. Once you're driving, you can then figure out how to steer and handle whatever problems arise.

The key, therefore, is to avoid letting preparation become the business. In other words, don't be *that person*.

Which person?

You may not know him by name, but you've undoubtedly seen him. *That person*. He has a way of ending up at the networking events for nearly every industry.

My first thought was that he shows up for the free food. Until I saw him at events where there wasn't any.

So why is *that person* at the networking events?

She's there to live vicariously through others who have actual businesses. You see, *that person* has never started her own business. She's never taken the plunge. But you'd never suspect it from the way she talks.

I found this out personally at real estate networking events. *That person* showed up and proceeded to talk REI like a pro. His knowledge was so airtight that I assumed he'd done many deals. Only later did I learn he'd never bought or sold any real estate. Ever.

My first reaction upon learning the truth was disappointment, because I'd actually saved his business card and intended to follow up with him.

The disappointment I felt, though, was probably nothing compared to the disappointment *that person* feels. She may not show it outwardly, but deep down it's probably disappointing for her to not be an actual business owner. This would explain why she gets a contact high off being around people with real businesses. That high lets her escape from the painful reality of having not started her own business.

The moral of the story? Don't be *that person*.

How do you avoid being *that person*?

You Just Start.

There's that phrase again, Just Start. Hope you like the way it sounds. Because you're going to be hearing it a lot in the pages ahead. It's the fundamental theme of this book, underlying everything else.

Just Start.

In the context of this book, that means giving yourself permission to finally start your own business, recognizing the need to execute, without being reckless nor delaying action forever with education.

Just Start.

It's also an applicable message for those who are currently in business and looking to take things to that clichéd next level. For those of you in this second group, please stick around even when the material seems geared primarily to newbies. You — the experienced business owners — will also find lots of actionable ideas and concepts in the upcoming chapters.

Just Start.

It's the core message of this book. But it's also not the only thing we're going to talk about. No, definitely not.

Our discussion is also going to cover the tactics for once you're moving. Meaning, you'll learn what to do and what to focus on once you've actually gotten started. Those tactics, however, will purposely be kept to a minimum. They'll also be presented in a way that doesn't give you 500+ things to think about.

My rationale in presenting tactics this way is that I don't want you to slip back into analysis paralysis. Which is exactly what might happen if I give you a list of tactics that's size XXXL. A list that big won't help you get started. So let's keep things nice and manageable with a respectable, yet not overwhelming number of tactics.

As for those tactics, you'll find them split out across six core concepts. Those six concepts are the meat of this book. And they're not just abstract thoughts. Instead, each of them was instrumental in helping me explode my businesses to multi-million dollar levels.

That success came, however, after I'd wasted years. Five of those years were wasted on preparing to start a business. You know, going to seminars, reading books, watching YouTube videos. Then, once I finally started my business, I wasted another five years trying to figure it all out without any guidance, carefully planning how to scale.

Anyway, you get the idea. You need to Just Start, and then the six core concepts will help you once your business actually exists.

Here's a preview of the concepts:

Core Concept #1: Hiring

Think hiring's only for companies like IBM and Ford? I did too early on. As a new business owner, I felt that hiring didn't make sense for me, given the size of my business and its revenue at the time. Only later did I realize how to hire people in ways that are creative, cost-effective, and ethical. Those ways of hiring will be covered in this first section.

Core Concept #2: Culture and Team-Building

These terms, culture and team-building, may sound irrelevant given that you're not yet running a Fortune 500 company. But even on a small scale, you're still dealing with other people, those people being the ones you hire for your team with the help of Core Concept #1.

With that in mind, you need a company culture that supports employees and allows them to do their best work. Along with culture, you also need everyone in your organization to feel united as a team.

And no, these aren't someday items either. They're things you need to concentrate on right now. Fail to do that and you'll find yourself, as I did, with a toxic employee who's destroying your entire company. My particular story involved a toxic employee who had excellent job skills, yet definitely didn't play well with others. The story of this employee is a cautionary tale for you and you'll be hearing all about it in Core Concept #2.

Core Concept #3: Why?

What motivates you in starting and then running your business? Maybe you know. Or perhaps you're unclear about it. We'll be covering how to find and sharpen your own sense of Why in this third core concept.

In addition, we'll also be talking about the other, far-less talked about Why. This would be the Why of your company. Why do your employees feel motivated to come to work each day and contribute their best efforts? There are definite reasons for that, and if you don't know or don't like the ones at your company, Core Concept #3 may just be your favorite one.

Core Concept #4: Partnering

No discussion of being an entrepreneur would be complete without covering partnerships. We'll address them here, helping you answer the question of whether you actually need a partner. In the process, you'll also hear about a painful, yet all too common force driving many partnerships.

Core Concept #5: Maintenance

You'll need to continually monitor and maintain everything we covered in the first four core concepts. Otherwise your progress will eventually erode, leaving you back at square one. To avoid that, you'll therefore need to monitor what's going on with respect to each of the previous four core concepts. And at the same time, you'll want to perform maintenance based on what you find from monitoring.

An example of monitoring and maintenance would be in the area of company culture. You may realize that your employees don't feel like they can relax and have a good time when you, their boss, are around. Or you might realize that you have a toxic employee, as I mentioned earlier. These two situations need to be remedied, yet you might be unaware of them without careful monitoring and subsequent maintenance.

How do you practice monitoring and maintenance? All will be revealed in Core Concept #5.

Core Concept #6: Mentors

This last core concept might surprise you, and I'm not going to ruin the surprise. But I promise you one thing. While the discussion will involve mentors, it won't be some cheesy, thinly-veiled sales pitch. Put another way, you won't reach the end of the chapter and find an offer to buy into some mentorship program. Frankly, that would be manipulative crap in my humble opinion, and I won't subject you to it. Instead, you can look forward to a frank and eye-opening look at mentors, one that leaves you feeling empowered rather than used.

*

OK, ready to roll? It's almost time.

Almost time for you and I to head into the rest of this book.

And almost time, once this book is over, for you to Just Start.

But before that, I have a few quick things to get off my chest.

First of all, this book assumes you want to scale a business. That could mean scale from a brand new company into something larger, or grow an existing company. That's my assumption, but maybe it's not where you're at. Maybe you want to be a one-man band, the kind of business owner whose venture keeps the lights on, pays the bills, and nothing more. Like a lawn company, for example, where the owner also cuts all the lawns.

If that's the case, follow your heart. But don't follow me into the rest of this book. It's not written for you. My focus is on scaling and that's the context for all the upcoming material here. So if you're content to be a one-man band, save yourself time and stop reading.

As in right now.

Another thing we need to be absolutely clear about now is excuses. If you're the type who makes excuses, you should be terrified. For this book will leave you with no excuses for not taking action. Not only will you get permission to Just Start, but you'll also learn a manageable number of tactics for after you have started. With those things covered, what excuses are left? Need for more knowledge? Nope.

What's left at that point? Nothing. No excuses, no real ones anyway.

Oh, and please don't give me the "you had special advantages" line. I don't want to come off as shrill, but I had no special advantages. In fact, my first company was started with many disadvantages. There were ironclad chains around my mind about entrepreneurship, having been in the corporate world and raised by two decidedly non-entrepreneurial parents. Additionally, and perhaps more relevant to you, I had three kids, a mortgage, and a full-time job at the time I created my first company. This is why I'll keep saying until I'm blue in the face: if I can start a business and scale it into millions of dollars, you can absolutely do it too.

Lastly, do yourself a favor, and give this book your undivided attention. Don't try and read this book while also consuming scores of other media. Doing that will only dilute the material we're about to cover. You'll be overwhelmed with ideas despite my efforts in this book to help you avoid that feeling. Don't do it. Make this book your focus until you finish reading it. It's not a long book either, nothing like *Crime and Punishment* or *War and Peace*. So give it a chance. Practice book monogamy, if you will.

That's all I've got, at least for the introduction. Let's head on into the first of our core concepts: hiring.

Chapter 1 - Hiring

"An army of one."

What comes to mind when you read that?

If you're like me, you probably think of action heroes, men and women on the big screen who are tough as nails and can take on the world by themselves. Guys like Arnold Schwarzenegger or Chuck Norris, the original army of one in the movie of the same name. Women too, like Sigourney Weaver in the *Alien* movies or Uma Thurman in *Kill Bill*.

But the point is not to geek out.

Because this isn't ultimately about action movies.

No, it's about that idea of the army of one, and how, contrary to what you might expect, being an army of one is not always a good thing. In fact, when it comes to business, being an army of one means you're actually quite weak and at a serious disadvantage. So it isn't something to celebrate. Nor is it something to pound your chest and feel badass about.

Instead, as a business owner, you should dread the thought of being an army of one. And you should avoid it like the plague, if you truly want to grow.

Right now, though, you may be unclear about why it's essential not to be an army of one. In the interest of clarity, let's dive into that now.

To begin with, think about how limiting it is to run a business by yourself. If it's just you, the company's accomplishments are limited to whatever you, personally, can get done. Assuming you've got the same 24 hours in a day as I do, then you'll likely see the problem. There simply isn't enough time to do everything you want or need to do to grow your business at the rate, or to the size, that you desire.

But wait, you say. What about productivity? Life hacks, 80-20, and other cutting-edge ways for a person to get more done than would otherwise seem possible. What about all of that? Surely there's some kind of rebuttal, something to suggest that perhaps it is possible to be an army of one.

Sadly, that's not the case. An army of one can be schooled in all the latest productivity tricks and tactics. Yet such an individual is still just that: an individual. And as an individual, they're still limited in terms of what they alone can ultimately accomplish.

The bottom line is that you don't want to be an army of one. Instead, you want to be the leader of a full-on army of employees. Having this army will enable you to scale your business and overcome your own personal limitations.

How do you hire employees or build your army? In the pages ahead, we'll discuss hiring in depth, thereby equipping you to confidently recruit and onboard the right employees for your business.

This chapter won't just be a technical discussion of hiring, though. For that's just one aspect, arguably the least important. In discussing hiring, what's most important is the mental aspect. I'm referring here to the limiting beliefs that prevent business owners from hiring.

The mental side is of such importance that any serious discussion of hiring needs to start there. So let's do that. Let's talk about all the head trash that holds business owners back in their hiring efforts.

The first thing you should know is that it's not just you. Nearly all of us face mental obstacles, to some extent, when it comes to hiring. I'm no exception.

In fact, I was probably worse at it than you are. In my case, I didn't even think about hiring. It took me five long years to realize I needed to hire. Crazy, right? I mean, imagine you're in business and not getting anywhere, and you don't think that maybe, just maybe, hiring might be the solution. That's where I was, for the better part of five years.

Not that I realized it during that time. No, I was firmly convinced that there had to be some other explanation, something I needed to figure out in order to take my business to the proverbial next level. What that something else was, I couldn't say. But it couldn't be related to hiring. Not when I was the army of one, able to kick ass and take names in my business efforts.

So I fought on, practically killing myself working on my business, yet unable to achieve any meaningful growth.

Clichéd as it sounds, I felt as though I were spinning on one of those hamster wheels. The harder I worked on my business, the harder I worked on my business.

How's that for motivation? It doesn't exactly leave you energized and eager to work each day.

Equally demotivating was the reaction I got from my peers at the time. Nearly all of them honestly thought that I was successful.

Deep down, though, I didn't feel successful. Because if I were truly succeeding, my business would be growing, and I wouldn't be on the hamster wheel.

Reading this now, you're probably wondering what finally clicked. What was it that finally opened my eyes to hiring as the answer?

Looking back, I wish I could say exactly. But my memory on how the breakthrough happened is pretty hazy. So I can't say there was a moment when, like Isaac Newton, I saw an apple fall and instantly had a revelation. Nor was there a moment when I suddenly jumped up, yelled, "Eureka," and instantly knew that hiring was it. If anything like that happened, well I certainly can't remember it.

What I do remember, however, is the aftermath. I realized on a gut level that being a one-man army was what had held me back in business.

Following that realization, my business exploded. I won't bore you with the growth stats or brag about my financials. All I'll say is that business became very good. Good enough that my friends were finally justified in calling me successful.

Despite having broken through, I can't forget the uphill battle that preceded it. It sucked, quite frankly. And I'd hate for you to experience anything similar. The only way to avoid that, however, is to crush whatever limiting beliefs you have about employees and hiring. You and I can do that by working together in this chapter, like a tag team in wrestling, to knock out all those things in your mind that prevent you from hiring.

Here are the five most common limiting beliefs that prevent new entrepreneurs from hiring:

1. Hiring is a luxury

2. Now is not the right time to hire

3. You don't have enough money to hire.

4. Your employees won't be as good at their given tasks as you are.

5. Your employees won't have as much passion as you do.

1. Hiring is a Luxury

The first limiting belief that we need to knock out is that hiring is a luxury. Business owners with this belief view hiring as something that's nice to do, something they'll get around to doing later.

If that's where your head's at, I've got news for you. Hiring is definitely not a luxury. It's an element essential for real growth. Without it, your business will absolutely positively not grow beyond a point. And if your business isn't growing, it's dying.

Let me repeat that so it really sinks in.

If your business isn't growing, it's dying.

Dying. Not standing still. Not keeping pace. No, dying. It's really that simple. As simple as yes or no, on or off, hot or cold, and a multitude of other binary things in life.

Given the simplicity of the growth versus dying idea, you probably don't need me to say any more about it. The idea is probably clear in your mind. You understand the importance of growing your business and how hiring contributes to growth.

And yet, you still may not hire employees.

Why not?

I can't speak for you personally. But having coached countless business owners, here's what I can say. If you still refrain from hiring at this point, it's probably because you have one of four remaining limiting beliefs about hiring.

2. Now is Not the Right Time to Hire

The second of those limiting beliefs is a close cousin of the hiring is a luxury idea. It's the belief that now is not the right time to hire.

If you've got this belief, you may really want to hire. But each time you think about hiring, you tell yourself that it's just not the right time. You've got too many things on your plate right now. Or the market your business operates in needs to improve first. Or other conditions are in play that you cite as proof that now's just not the right time to hire employees for your business.

Say what you will, but deep down you probably know that there's rarely a perfect time to do anything. If you're a parent, for example, were you able to cherry-pick the absolute best possible time to have kids? Probably not. Life typically doesn't work that way. Not with kids and not when it comes to business matters like hiring. So rid yourself of this flawed idea that everything's got to be ideal in order for you to hire. It's not going to happen. Your ducks, so to speak, will never all be in a row. The traffic lights will never all be green at once. The market will never be 100% ideal.

Another thing that probably won't be ideal is the size of your business. I hear this one quite often from other business owners, including those I coach. They sometimes think that there's a magic size a business must grow to before hiring makes sense.

Yet what is that magic size? The average business owners — or at least those I've talked to — usually don't know. All they can say is that their business needs to be bigger before they can hire.

Bigger, but by how much? Plus, what is the idea of big even based on? Is it based on profits, clients/customers, reach, or something else?

Even if you've got an answer to what big means, the notion of not being big enough to hire is still invalid and even ironic. The irony is that you're not big enough to hire, but in fact, you'll never be big unless you *do* hire. It's circular reasoning, a catch-22.

On top of that, let me also point out that there's a critical mass your business needs to hit within its first few years. For the sake of simplicity, I'll define this critical mass as the speed you need to reach in order to get your business off the ground so it doesn't die. Critical mass does vary depending on the exact nature of your business. Yet in all cases, looking at critical mass will show you whether your business is indeed growing versus dying.

Let's not get caught up, though, in exhaustively defining critical mass. The bigger idea is that whatever critical mass is for your business, you don't have a prayer of reaching it unless you hire.

This is why you need to think about hiring from day one. In other words, the day you start your business, you need to also be thinking about who you're going to hire. Your thoughts should be guided by your vision of the next two to three years. Figure out what you want to achieve with your business in that time, and then look at who you'll need to hire to achieve it.

As you're figuring these things out, I recommend building an organizational chart. An organizational chart, or "org chart," shows who will be in your company and what roles they'll be filling.

With the org chart, it's best to focus only on the next two to three years. That's a manageable and realistic timeframe to plan for. It won't overwhelm you like planning for the next thirty-five or fifty years might.

Build your org chart and build it now. This way you'll have a clear plan to follow as you build your company. You'll know exactly what positions will eventually need to be filled. You'll also avoid bringing people on in a haphazard, ad hoc way that just makes a mess.

Business owners often wind up with such a mess when they lack a clear, long-term blueprint for who needs to be hired. That blueprint, of course, is your org chart. It serves as the map of your company, depicting how the company's going to be built. You need such a map from day one, as silly as that might sound. This is because a map helps you know who you're going to put where and how you'll grow your business over the long-haul, and therefore what steps you need to take from the beginning.

All this talk about an org chart and long-term planning may sound great, but it seems to overlook a major elephant in the room, namely money.

Assuming you aren't planning to run a sweatshop, anyone you hire will need to be paid money. But where will that money come from? And do you have enough?

3. You Don't Have Enough Money to Hire

Facing questions like that, you may succumb to another limiting belief around hiring: that you don't have enough money to hire.

Of all the limiting beliefs on hiring, I personally find this one to be the saddest. It saddens me to see business owners underestimate themselves like this. They're creative enough and resourceful enough to start businesses. Yet at the same time, these business owners feel powerless in coming up with the money to hire employees.

If you're in that position, I'd encourage you to give yourself more credit. Stop underestimating your abilities, especially your imagination and creativity. Money doesn't have to be an insurmountable obstacle that prevents you from hiring. The key is to think outside the so-called box to figure out how you can afford to hire.

Here's a question that can help you do that: How can you structure someone's compensation so they'll take the job and their work supports you and your business goals?

That question would allow you to get creative, for example, in hiring sales staff. In the case of sales, you might find commission to be your solution. Sales professionals often work on commission and you could conceivably use the same compensation with your own hires. So you'd bring someone on for sales who'd work either fully or partly on commission.

Creative thinking about compensation might also lead you to consider geo arbitrage. This is the idea of hiring people in another country to work for you at what's considered a fair wage in their country.

An example of geo arbitrage might be hiring someone in the Philippines to make cold calls for your company at the rate of $4 per hour. Whoever you hired in this case might be completely competent and able to do quality work. In addition, the $4 per hour might be a competitive wage by that employee's local standards, meaning that you're not exploiting them. You're simply getting comparable quality work from outside the U.S. at a decidedly cheaper rate.

While we're on sales, let me suggest another idea around compensation. It's what I do with the employees in my businesses. I make sure everyone in the company has some portion of their compensation tied to profitability. This way, we can all be excited about our wins, while at the same time being conscious of the company's profits.

As an illustration, consider the role of transaction coordinator. This is the person on my team who works with title companies to get properties we're buying to the closing table. I mention this job because it's an administrative position. My transaction coordinator isn't on the cutting edge of sales and is seemingly removed from much of the company profitability.

How then, could this employee's compensation be tied to profitability in a meaningful way such that when our company has a big win, this person is also able to participate in the win, with compensation directly tied to it?

The solution I found was to adjust the transaction coordinator's compensation so it now has a salary plus a profit-sharing component. This solution came through creative thinking, so it gives further credence to creativity as a means of overcoming the money obstacle in hiring.

If you can get past the perceived money obstacle, overcoming that limiting belief about hiring, then you can create your org chart. A salesperson might be among the first people in the chart, but you can't assume that. Instead, I recommend you take a better approach to determining who goes in your org chart and who your first hires will be.

In recommending the following approach, I'm assuming your business has just started and is not a mature company. Maybe that's obvious to you since we're discussing your first hires. But if not, now you know.

As you do your org chart and plan initial hiring, keep your eyes firmly fixed on the present. This is not the time to hire for the next thirty years. Instead, think about who you need to hire right now to assist with immediate responsibilities in your business. Your thinking should be guided by two criteria.

First, think about the aspects of your business that you're unskilled in or don't enjoy doing. Then, once you have a clear sense of those things, you can hire someone to do them for you.

As an example, consider what I did with sales. Sales happen to be an area I'm weak in. I may also be the only business owner in the world who doesn't enjoy doing sales calls. Absurd as it might sound, I don't like hopping on a call and trying to sell someone a product or service.

My weakness in sales and the fact that I don't enjoy it gave me absolute clarity in hiring. As you might expect, my first hire — the first person as well, in the org chart — was a salesperson. I found a true sales pro, someone who was great at selling and loved doing it.

The person I hired for sales began working for me part time. He ended up doing such a great a job that we eventually became business partners.

You may or may not end up with a similar result from hiring, gaining a business partner as I did. Yet even if that doesn't happen, you'll still be better off, since in this first case, you'll be spared from work that you either don't enjoy, aren't skilled at, or both.

The second criteria, when hiring for immediate needs at the start of your business, is in regards to bottlenecks. When you think in these terms, you realize you're hiring someone to help you overcome a bottleneck in your business.

Bottleneck simply means a point of congestion in your business, a point where things get clogged up, causing your business to function poorly or perhaps not at all.

The irony of a bottleneck is that, as a business owner, you're usually well aware of what it is. That's because the bottleneck is usually you.

You, yes you, are typically the bottleneck in your business. Once this sinks in, you'll be able to hire accordingly. Provided you're indeed the bottleneck, you can hire people to help you get out of the way. This in turn will unclog the business and increase revenues.

Then again, you might not be the bottleneck. It could be that someone else in your business is the true source of the clog.

How can you be certain about who's the bottleneck?

The simple way is to look at your efforts versus revenue. If you're working as hard as you can and revenues aren't increasing the way you want, then you're the bottleneck. You therefore have no choice but to hire if you want to meet your revenue goals.

Hiring cures bottlenecks. Remember that so you don't waste time trying to fix a bottleneck just by working harder.

I made that mistake early on in my business. In those days, I hit a ceiling with revenue. Try as I might, the revenue for my business just wouldn't increase. And believe me, I tried. I worked harder and harder and harder, putting in the kind of hours that would make an overworked investment banker cringe. Not that I was earning anything close to what an investment banker would earn. But I certainly put in comparably lengthy and exhausting work weeks.

This was hard, hard work, and at the end of it all, guess what the result was? Had my business attained jaw-dropping revenues and reached a level where we might take the company public with an IPO?

No, of course not. Revenues had increased, but not proportional to the amount of hours I was working. And there was certainly no IPO in the works.

I learned the hard way that bottlenecks are cured through hiring as opposed to just putting in more hours. That's my message to you as you consider the second criteria for making your initial hiring decisions.

I want you to become a strategist versus a worker bee. As a strategist, you see your business as though it were a chessboard. Then, like Bobby Fischer, the 1980s chess champion, you move the pieces around the chessboard with a cool precision, taking down the opposition and ultimately putting your revenue goals in checkmate.

Exciting, right? Attainable too. But only if you hire people.

Also, don't let the notion of being a strategist fool you. Hiring is necessary regardless of how masterful a strategist you are or how much genius you possess.

If you want proof, just look at two of the most successful entrepreneurs in recent history, Steve Jobs and Steve Wozniak, or "Woz."

Jobs was a master strategist when it came to sales, but not nearly as hot with engineering. Woz was a genius engineer, but couldn't sell his way out of a box. Together, they made up for one another's weaknesses, achieving some initial success. Then, to truly change the world, taking a little company called Apple to the heights it's achieved today, they hired countless others. How's that for compelling evidence of why you should hire?

Speaking of Jobs and Woz, there's a good chance the people you hire won't have as much genius or talent as they did. Few of us get that lucky. But then you don't need to have employees who are as prodigious as Apple's founders.

4. Your Employees Won't Be as Good at Their Given Tasks as You Are

I mention that because it connects to another limiting belief. The limiting belief here is that you can't hire because your employees won't be as good at their given tasks as you are. This belief is blatantly wrong if you're hiring, as I mentioned earlier, based on what you're unskilled at. But it's also wrong when hiring for those tasks you're good or even excellent at. In this second case, the limiting belief has no basis because you don't usually need to hire someone who's as skilled as you are.

Instead, what you probably need is just an employee who's good enough. Good enough will get the job done now, and you can always upgrade later, hiring a truly exceptional employee down the road.

The employees you hire may get the job done at good enough or even rock star levels, but will they really care?

5. Your Employees Won't Have the Same Level of Passion as You

This question brings us to the last of the major limiting beliefs about hiring. We're talking now about concern over apathy. Business owners with this belief worry that anyone they hire won't have the same level of passion and commitment to the company as they the business owner has.

To overcome this limiting belief, especially if you're personally struggling with it, I suggest acknowledging the obvious, that you're right. Your employees probably won't care nearly as much as you do. Moreover, no one — employees or otherwise — will care about your company to the same extent as you do. But that's true for every company that's ever been created.

Take Apple, the company we recently talked about. Apple's founders Jobs and Woz had inherently more passion and commitment to the company than any of their employees. Yet that difference in passion and commitment didn't mean the two founders couldn't hire. And fortunately for Mac lovers everywhere, Jobs and Woz did hire.

Take a lesson from Apple and accept that you alone are going to be the most enthusiastic about your business.

At the same time, though, recognize that your employees also don't have the same investment in the company as you do. Since you're the founder/owner, your investment in the company will naturally be the greatest of anyone there. Provided you don't have a business partner, no one else at your company will have nearly the same emotional and financial stake as you do.

Is it really a surprise then that your employees won't share your level of enthusiasm?

Not really. And you can't expect them to either. So stop thinking you have to find employees who'd join you in metaphorically cutting off both their legs for your business. You simply don't need that level of devotion. Maybe you would if you were Jim Jones, running a Kool-Aid drinking cult. But you're not. You can get by just fine with an employee who'd only cut off their right arm for the company.

All this talk about passion and dedication rests on the assumption, though, that you do indeed care about your company. I take it as a given that you care, with an intensity others lack. If this isn't the case, and your employees care more about the company than you do, then perhaps you need to do some soul-searching. It may be time to seriously reconsider whether you should even be in business.

But you care, don't you?

If so, let's move on.

We're done discussing the limiting beliefs around hiring. Having smashed through them, it's time for us to concentrate on actionable how-to's. We're going to look at how exactly you go about hiring people. I've laid out a simple six-step process that will give you everything you need to hire the right people for your company.

1. Always be recruiting

2. Post the job and get the word out

3. Review résumés

4. 10-minute initial phone interviews

5. First face-to-face interviews

6. Second face-to-face interviews

Step 1: Always Be Recruiting

Step one in the how of hiring is a simple principle: always be recruiting.

Recruiting means being on the lookout for talent. You may not want or need to hire this talent just yet. But you're always, always looking to find it.

This principle of always being in recruiting mode is comparable to baseball. Look at the major league teams and you'll see that they're often supported by minor league teams. These minor league teams provide a stock of players from which those in the majors can draw as they build their rosters.

It's no different for you as a business owner. You should have your own equivalent of a minor league team, a pool of talented candidates where you can find employees when you need them.

The people in your talent pool are interested in working for you, yet you haven't offered them a job. You may do that, eventually, but that's not important for the time being.

What matters here and now is that you know you could call those in your talent pool up to the big leagues if you needed to, if, for example, one of your employees left, the company creating a vacancy, or if your finances ever permitted the addition of extra employees.

In either of those scenarios, your talent pool would be an invaluable asset. So make sure you have a talent pool. The way to do that is, as I said earlier, is to always be recruiting.

Always be recruiting means always be recruiting.

Like always.

Not just today or this quarter. Not just next quarter either when you launch some spiffy new initiative.

Always. You need to always be recruiting. Otherwise, you make the same blunder as business owners often do in sales. This is the mistake of not doing sales until it's do-or-die urgent, perhaps with the company about to go out of business. The same urgency can arise with recruiting if you're suddenly scrambling to fill a position to keep your business afloat.

Avoid that kind of anxiety by recruiting constantly. Take the time now to begin recruiting and building your talent pool of interested warm prospects. It'll be worthwhile later, I promise.

Step 2: Post the Job and Get the Word Out

Recruiting for the future is fine, but at some point you'll need to actually hire people.

When that need arises and you're hiring for the here-and-now, the key is to get the word out. Make your hiring needs known to as many people as possible. The more people who know you're hiring, the more candidates you'll have for the roles you're looking to fill.

How do you get the word out? One effective method is social media. It's a great way to publicize your hiring needs to a large audience who may then spread the message virally to countless other people.

Along with social media, you can also employ more traditional methods to get the word out about your company's hiring needs. Those include online recruiting sites like ZipRecruiter, Indeed, and Craigslist.

Craigslist? Yes, Craigslist. Unlikely as it may seem, Craigslist can still be a source from which to draw employees. This depends in part on what you're hiring for. Don't rule Craigslist out. It can often surprise you, producing highly qualified applicants.

You may be just as surprised — in a good way — if you turn to an outsourcing website. These are sites where you can hire workers from overseas to perform contracted tasks or even full-on jobs. I alluded to these earlier, when we talked about using creativity to overcome the financial hurdles around hiring.

Among the outsourcing websites, Upwork is by far the largest. It's not the only one, however. You can find countless other outsourcing websites, platforms, and overall hiring solutions out there if you do a simple search.

Another example is Fiverr, a site where you hire people to do small temporary gigs for just $5. Another would be TopTal, a hiring platform built specifically for the tech industry.

If outsourcing doesn't work for you, you might turn to a headhunter. It's yet another option when hiring.

Whether you use a headhunter or any other hiring sources I've described, the point is to get the word out. Getting the word out is what matters most. How you do it can be refined as you go.

Focus on publicizing your hiring needs. Stop overthinking and start bringing in all the applicants you possibly can.

Once the applicants begin rolling in, you need to determine who you'll consider for the position. You can get a head start on that in your job postings. Include a requirement in the posting for applicants to do at least one thing up front.

Applicants could, for instance, be required to write the phrase "hire me now" in their cover letter. Having a requirement like this would enable you to quickly see who followed your directions and who didn't. With the "hire me now" example, you could quickly discard any applications that didn't include that key phrase. The people who submitted those applications wouldn't be worth considering, since they clearly didn't follow directions.

Of those applicants who did follow your directions, you could then screen them based on an industry question or criteria. An example would be whether the applicant has at least one year of sales experience. I've used that same question to great success with applicants from the recruiting website Indeed.com.

The question I've asked here about sales experience works because it provides a second litmus test that, like "hire me now," expedites my efforts in sifting through applications. You don't have to use my exact question, though, and chances are you shouldn't either. Pick your own, but feel free to leverage it as I have, to find sanity amidst what may seem like an overwhelming sea of job applications.

Step 3: Review Résumés

After you've screened your applicants, it's time to review résumés.

In this step, you'll look at the résumés of those applicants who clearly have half a brain, or at least enough of a brain to follow directions and pass your initial qualification. You alone know what you're looking for, so I'll leave reviewing the résumés up to you.

Step 4: 10-Minute Initial Phone Interviews

It makes more sense for me to guide you in Step 4 of the hiring process. Step 4 is where you briefly interview each candidate you're considering. The initial interview only lasts 10 minutes and it's done over the phone. This gives you a sense of the remaining applicants without investing too much time and energy.

When doing these initial 10-minute phone interviews, you just want applicants to talk. That's it. Get them to open up a bit so you can see who they are beyond the written application.

To get applicants talking, I recommend asking simply, "Is there anything from your résumé that you'd like to clarify or explain?"

I've asked this question so much that I'm almost sick of it. Yet I can't let the question go because it's very powerful. Chances are you'll have the same reaction once you employ this question or a similar one in your own hiring efforts.

It's staggering to see how a question like this causes people to let their guard down and reveal things that instantly disqualify them from consideration.

Wondering what an applicant might say that would be so troubling? Here's an example. I've heard different versions of this response on a number of occasions when doing the 10-minute initial interview.

Following my question, the applicant says that he's had so many jobs because all of his past bosses were idiots.

All of them were idiots? Right. Well, no need to work for another idiot. And with that, I promptly discard the candidate without any further consideration.

Here's a script for the phone interview. This way you'll have a leg up when it comes time to write your own.

The script is as follows:

Start of Script

"We're doing 10 minute phone interviews in advance. Is there anything you'd like to share that's not on your résumé but that's relevant for this position, or is there anything you'd like to highlight from your résumé that you feel is important?"

End of Script

Wait, is that it? The entire script? Just those two sentences?

Yes, that's the script all right, every last bit of it. And yes, to the untrained eye, it may look small.

Yet despite its size, this script packs a big punch. It's sort of like the Manny Pacquiao of interview scripts.

Pacquaio, if you'll recall, is the internationally acclaimed welterweight boxing champion. The guy's 5'5 and weighs about 145 pounds, hardly a giant by any stretch of the imagination. But you definitely would not want to get in the way of his fist. The same goes for this script. Small but deadly, like the little friend Al Pacino's enemies say hello to in the film *Scarface*.

Suffice to say, this script more than makes up for its brevity. Its magic lies in giving your applicants an opening at the end. You set the stage by offering them the chance to elaborate. Then, with that opening available, you sit back and watch as those applicants with skeletons in their closets proceed to hang themselves.

Applicants may do this during your initial interview, but you still need to keep a straight face. Stay professional and wear a so-called poker face. That means you'll end the phone interviews neutrally. As the interviews finish, tell the applicants you'll be in touch if you decide a face-to-face interview, the next step, makes sense.

Step 5: First Face-to-Face Interviews

The first face-to-face interview is Step 5 of my hiring process. This in-person interview is the first of two that you'll be doing. I recommend that the first face-to-face interview be conducted by a decision-maker other than the one they'd be reporting to if hired.

If you're the one the applicant would report to as an employee, you should sit this first interview out. One of your colleagues should do the interview in your place. Otherwise, there's too much risk that you, as the applicant's eventual manager, will "fall in love" with him too soon and making bad hiring decisions. This risk is mitigated by having a non-manager do the first round face-to-face interviews.

Step 6: Second Face-to-Face Interviews

In this second round of face-to-face interviews, it's your turn as manager. This is the point where you can come in and meet the survivors, the top two to three most qualified people who remain at this point in the hiring process. Meet these survivors and make your assessment of which one would be best for you to hire and manage as an employee.

If you're not the one who will be managing the new hire, then you'll be absent from this step, participating in the Step 5 interview instead.

*

Even as you focus on hiring with the steps outlined here, it's important to also consider the other side of the equation, the opposite of hiring, which is firing.

Now, if you're like most business owners, you're not exactly eager to fire people. In fact, you may be so reluctant that you'd prefer the pain of a firing squad to the pain of having to fire an employee.

Despite the pain, though, firing is often necessary. There's no getting around that. Sorry. Wish I could tell you differently, but it's just not so. What I can do, however, is give you a bit of guidance to make firing less of a challenge.

The first thing I can about firing is that you need the right perspective. Without the right perspective, you may mistakenly fire someone, letting go of a person who should in fact be kept on.

To avoid that mistake, be a realist. In other words, make sure you focus on what is rather than what should be. You need to look solely at the facts. When you do that, you see things as they are, no better and no worse.

Here's an example of how to do that. Consider an employee of yours who's not measuring up to the demands of her position. Your own assumption is that the employee should be able to do what's required for the given role. Yet since that's not happening, you may need to reexamine the position and determine if it's possible for anyone to measure up.

For example, in my business, I delegated some tasks to an employee who wasn't getting the job done. Finally, I cornered her and she told me she was falling asleep at her keyboard every day. There was simply not enough time nor bandwidth in her day to complete everything I had been able to do. Expecting she could do what I had been able to do was unrealistic on my part because she wasn't the owner and didn't have the same incentive as I did.

Additionally, in this example, make sure you don't fall prey to the "I can do it" trap. This is the scenario where a business owner measures employees against that business owner's own personal capabilities. Owners who falter here think, "Well, I could certainly do this job. Why can't my employee?" In doing so, these owners see the individual employee as the problem and don't consider whether the job description itself needs to be modified.

I'm personally guilty of having made this mistake. In my business, I used to stress what should be happening, especially with my employees. Rather than facing the facts, I interpreted my employees' failure to measure up as evidence that they weren't trying hard enough.

It seemed ridiculous to me, in those days, that my own employees couldn't do what I was capable of doing. Only in time did I realize that I was overburdening my employees, overburdening them and handicapping myself too, with an inanely stubborn view of how things should be.

Should. Should. Should.

Ok, but what if they really are the problem?

What if your employee really isn't doing her best? What if it is his fault? What if you really are justified in saying, "It's not me, it's you." And you're equally justified in firing them.

What then?

Provided you are 100% correct, then yes, you probably should fire that employee. But there is a right way to go about doing it.

The right way involves having clear quantifiable goals in your company for each position that all employees are aware of. Having such goals allows your employees to know exactly where they stand and never be blindsided by termination.

Getting blindsided won't happen when all employees in the company have visible and easily attainable goals they're working toward each week. Have a weekly meeting at which your employees then report on whether or not they met their goal. This way, the goal and the employees' performance in relationship to it are publicly visible.

Such visibility ensures that when one of your employees is terminated, everyone at the company can look back and understand why. They'll remember all the times when that person reported unacceptable results. No one will be surprised that he or she was let go. The employee himself probably won't be surprised either. She won't like getting fired. He might decorate the office with all kinds of colorful language on the way out. But you'll be able to give the person a quantifiable and clear reason for the firing.

The goals must also be relatively easily attainable. Goals that are easily attainable mean your employees can work without having to pull crazy hours and sacrifice their health in the process. This way, the terminated employee can't say that the goals were insurmountable.

The goals themselves should be numbers tied directly back to your company's revenue. Here's an example of how that would work. Suppose you wanted to make one million dollars in your business. You'd take that revenue target and divide it by fifty-two weeks in the year. Doing more math, you'd determine that each of your salespeople had to get two contracts per week times those fifty-two weeks. If your salespeople hit that target, you'd be on track to the goal of one million dollars in revenue. Conversely, if those in sales were only getting one contract per week, you would not be on course.

In both cases, there's a clear, mathematically linear correlation. That correlation allows you to know where things stand, and it also shows your employees that the goal itself is definitely not arbitrary. Employees know that there's a clear method to the madness.

Goals like a certain number of contracts each week make firing easier. So too does a policy of hire slow and fire fast. Hire slow means you don't rush to bring people onboard. You take your time, proceeding through the six-step hiring process we looked at earlier. That process will give you confidence that you're hiring the right people. Then, having a proper mindset and setting easily attainable and visible goals will help you confidently monitor your employees' progress.

Only then, at the end of it all, do you fire. And that's done fast, with "fast" being a relative term.

Let me shed some more light on firing for you by describing how we do it at my company. Those of us in managerial roles have those we supervise report to us on a weekly basis. What we see each week may be troubling. But we usually don't make any changes until the end of a given quarter.

In addition to the weekly look at our employees, we also provide performance reviews for everyone at the end of the year. The year-end assessment is referred to as a "positional evaluation" and it allows us to ensure everyone in the company is in the right role. We'll see, with the positional evaluation, whether the roles are indeed correct, or whether employees need to be shifted around to fill different roles in the coming year.

Assessments like this one can help you beyond determining who should occupy which roles in your company. They can also help you determine whether an employee is a good fit for your company's culture. Unfortunately that issue of fit sometimes doesn't show itself during the hiring process.

An employer may not place enough importance on hiring employees who are truly a fit for the company. The employer would only look at whether applicants did their previous jobs well, reviewing such things as skillsets and resume, while disregarding whether the applicant plays well with others.

But it might not be the employer's fault. The employee who gets hired might be such a good actor ("pathological liar" might be the better term) that he fools everyone into thinking he's a fit.

In either of these situations, you as an employer might only realize later on that the employee you'd hired isn't a fit and needs to be let go. Such a realization is possible when you assess employees on a regular basis, as described, looking at both their performance and their alignment with the culture of your company.

Related to the idea of fit is looking at both your applicants' and your employees' personalities and mindsets when assessing them. Those areas, personality and mindset, aren't going to be on anyone's résumé. How, then, do you judge these non-résumé, soft skill areas?

One way is to use tests like DISC and Kolbe. If you're unfamiliar with those tests, they're well worth looking into. I've personally used them to great success with my employees over the years. You won't believe the kind of insights, good and bad, that come when your employees take these kinds of tests. That's why I strongly recommend you use DISC, Kolbe, or something comparable with those in your company.

Tests can be invaluable, no question. But there's also a second way to judge your applicants and hires in the soft skill areas. This second way is simply listening to your gut. It's utterly unscientific, I'll admit, and you may worry about making a mistake. Still, your gut has a definite place in any decision about hiring and firing employees.

You can do all the phone screenings, interviews, assessment tests, and other things mentioned in this chapter. And you should do all of them. Yet you also need to listen to your gut. Without your gut feeling/reaction, you don't have a true 360-degree perspective about a person. Everything else helps, no question. But you must, must, must do a gut check too.

When you do that, if your gut is telling you that an applicant or employee is not a fit, listen to it. If you ignore your gut reaction, you may err as I did. My mistake was ignoring my gut and hiring an employee who eventually gutted my company, doing severe damage.

Listen to your gut when hiring and firing. But also make sure not to let the gut completely take over. It's all too easy to let a bad experience from ignoring your gut lead you to make decisions based only on gut reaction. I'm as bad as anyone at this, having hired solely based on the gut and also having hired solely based on skill sets. That's why I believe the key to hiring is to integrate both. Blend the two together and you'll be far more effective at judging your applicants and your employees as well.

*

Hopefully you're more confident now about hiring than when you began this chapter. You not only know that it's necessary, but you also understand how to do it.

As you might expect, there's a lot more information out there about hiring beyond the discussion in this book. Thousands of pages, hundreds of seminars and workshops, and millions of hits from a Google search.

None of that matters, though. Not right now. For if you'll recall from the first chapter, the problem isn't a lack of information. It's that all the information out there prevents you from ever getting started. The discussion here about hiring is all you need to know to get started with your business.

I'll conclude our discussion about hiring with an overall principle central to hiring: great leaders often credit their success to other people. The same will be true for you as an aspiring or established business owner. You got here because of you. But you'll get to where you want to be because of others. So who those others are matters. A lot.

Remember that as you think about hiring, and feel free to reread the chapter for additional inspiration. Then join me in the next chapter for a new look at the terms culture and team building.

Chapter 2 - Culture and Team Building

Tempting, isn't it?

To skip this chapter.

To give it a pass, to jump ahead to the other chapters which seem to hold far more useful material.

If you're thinking about doing that, I can't blame you.

In fact, I'd probably consider skipping this chapter too.

I mean, company culture?

Doesn't seem relevant.

Not when you're looking to Just Start in business, creating a new company or scaling an existing one.

If that's where you're at, what good is a chapter on company culture?

Such a chapter probably seems unhelpful, even a bit like filler.

It's comparable perhaps to when Richard Branson or some other billionaire business owner decides to give young, starving entrepreneurs the answer to building their businesses. This happens quite often when one of these business titans gives a keynote speech or sits on a conference panel.

In either of these situations, the billionaire will honestly volunteer what they believe is the answer. The key. The secret. That major game-changer that allowed him to achieve such jaw-dropping levels of success.

And you know what he says?

"Help people."

Or "Do your best."

Or "Enjoy the journey."

If you don't know what I'm talking about, look on YouTube. You'll find scores of videos where this happens. Videos where a well-meaning multi-millionaire business owner gives powerful advice that doesn't seem so powerful.

Look around on YouTube if you must, but then come back to this chapter. The one right here, on culture. It's worth reading, and I will prove that to you.

In the pages ahead, I'm going to show you why culture, the topic of this chapter, cannot be ignored. And, just as importantly, I'll be doing so in a way that satisfies your appetite for actionable answers.

So, I'm asking you to trust me.

Are you in?

If you are, then let's go.

To have a serious discussion on culture, the first thing we must do is define what it means with respect to business.

For our purposes here, culture can be defined as the personality of a company. Culture, in this sense, can be likened to each of our individual personalities.

Our individual personalities are our brands, shaping how people view us. The same goes for a company's culture.

In the company's case, culture becomes the brand, often quite literally, and it's this brand that influences people's perception of the company both internally, with employees, and externally, with the public.

An example of this is Google. As a company, it's created a search engine that a few people seem to like. Google's other claim to fame, though — one of many others — is having created a culture that's the envy of many a cubicle dweller.

Who wouldn't want to work at a company with a fun, youthful culture? A place where, for example, you're allowed to bring your dog to the office, and free gourmet lunch is the norm, not just a fun Friday thing.

Perks like those, and the culture that supports them, sound great. Not necessarily to those of us who want our own companies. But to the average employee? For them, Google is probably a place they'd sell a kidney to work. The be-all, end-all of employers.

See what Google's done? They've scored a grand slam, so to speak, in shaping people's perception, shaping perception to the point where Google has become synonymous with an enjoyable work environment.

Google's success with how they're perceived is dramatically illustrated in the following remark. It's one I heard a fellow employer say to his employees:

"This isn't Google. We don't do that here."

Now for the record, this employer has never worked at Google. Nor has he visited the "Google-plex," Google's sprawling corporate campus in Silicon Valley. I suspect too, that the employer doesn't even know any current or former Google employees.

Yet despite having no experience with the company, the employer I mentioned feels that he knows how things are done at Google.

That's the power of culture.

Culture isn't always positive, though. An example that's a total 180 degrees from Google would be Apple during the Steve Jobs era. Unlike Google, Apple under Jobs was a competitive, combative environment. This environment made working at Apple back in the day a nightmare experience for a majority of its employees. Many of Apple's employees back then, especially those reporting directly to Jobs, would probably never say they enjoyed being at work.

Apple's personality as a company, a.k.a. its culture, was that of a jerk. This isn't surprising, since Jobs himself is widely considered to have been a jerk to work for. His jerkiness as a person trickled down from the C-Suite like water and washed over the entire company. The result was a jerky culture.

Looking at Jobs in this example, we can see that a company's culture is an extension of its leader. If the leader is perceived as a jerk, the company will be too. The same goes for a company where the leader is all smiles and the epitome of friendliness.

There are, of course, plenty of personalities between these extremes too. Whatever the leader's personality, though, rest assured that it will drive or even determine the company culture.

Also, don't be misled by the fact that we've used Apple and Google as our examples. Those companies, large as they may be, are no different than the small company you may be starting, at least where culture is concerned.

In nearly all cases, the personality of the leader steering the company will set the tone for the overall culture at the company. Company size, therefore, is irrelevant.

If you want proof, think again about Apple. Despite the company having thousands of employees, Jobs' jerky personality still influenced the culture.

How then can we, as the owners of vastly smaller companies, expect our own personalities not to impact company culture?

We can't.

That's the fact of the matter, plain and simple.

Recognize it and act accordingly.

Oh, and one more point about Apple. For argument's sake, there probably were differences in culture by department. I'll admit that, as I don't want to just throw broad brushstrokes over Jobs-era Apple. And for the record, the jerky culture I described is in no way implying that Jobs, himself, was anything short of a genius, because in my opinion, he was.

So yes, at Apple and any other large company, there certainly can be varied cultures among the departments.

Even with the differences, however, it's worth pointing out that a company's owners are bound to hire people with the same attitudes and mindsets as themselves. It goes back to that terrible cliché that "Birds of a feather flock together." The cliché is terrible because it's simultaneously corny and all-too-true.

Birds of a feather do flock together, and we see this when looking at the leadership of departments in a company. Those leading the departments will have much the same temperament as the company's founders.

Thus, a company's culture is not safe, even in those departments seemingly removed from the jerky or tyrannical founder/owner.

The only way to keep those departments safe — truly safe — is to do as we're doing and discuss culture. Have an in-depth discussion about it, so there's no mystery in anyone's mind about the company culture and why it matters.

I can't say how that discussion will play out in your particular company. I can only comment on the importance of culture and why it matters.

This reason — a big one at that — can be summed up in a single term:

Millennials.

Know the term? It refers to that giant mass of kids born between about the mid-1980s to the year 2000.

Up until now, Millennials have indeed been kids. They've been in school and engaged in all of the issues that accompany student life.

Today, however, that's no longer the case. As of this writing in 2020, most Millennials are not kids in the literal sense in terms of their ages, nor in terms of their lifestyles.

Millennials are, for the most part, mature adults. This is evident when you examine what they're up to.

Take a look and you'll find Millennials getting married and starting families. You'll also find them entering the U.S. workforce in ever-increasing numbers.

Their entry into the workforce is what you and I care about because it's going to affect the way we hire and retain our employees.

We've already talked about hiring in the previous chapter. No need then, to rehash it here. The principles I've described in that chapter are Millennial-agnostic, meaning they'll work regardless of whether you're dealing with Millennials, senior citizens, Baby Boomers, or even Echo Boomers (those younger than Millennials). So we're good with hiring and can forgo discussion there.

What we do need to discuss, though, particularly in light of the Millennial generation, is employee retention. This is because unlike earlier generations, Millennials have decidedly different views of what's important at work. Their views matter to us as employers if we wish to retain our Millennial employees.

I say that about retaining Millennials like it's somehow optional. But it's not. Not when you think about the millions of Millennials who are now coming online as members of the workforce.

If you want to ignore them and their concerns, suit yourself. But I wouldn't. Especially when you consider the millions of Baby Boomers who are leaving the workforce for retirement. As they leave, the Baby Boomers are taking their views of what matters at work with them. What's left is the Millennials' perspective.

This perspective, how Millennials view the workplace, is bound to surprise you. In fact, you may need to pinch yourself like you were snapping out of a crazy dream when you see what Millennials feel is important at a job. Hint: it isn't money.

Money would certainly be at the top of the list for those of us who are older. Having been a proud member of the workforce, I'm all too aware of that. During my years as an employee, I was mostly focused on what a job paid, along with how much vacation time it allowed.

Millennials, however, don't see it this way. Money is, of course, still important to them. Vacations are too. But you know what Millennials usually rank ahead of those concerns?

Autonomy.

Autonomy? Yes. Millennials think autonomy is more important than how much money a job pays them.

Look, I know this sounds crazy. And to those of us in older generations (I'm a Gen X'er by the way), it is. But that's how Millennials — or at least a majority of them— see it.

My statements here about what Millennials want aren't just speculation. I'm basing those statements on two things.

The first is authoritative work torn from the pages of *INC. Magazine* and *Fast Company*.

In the case of *Inc. Magazine,* an article of theirs from 2015, "5 Surprising Things Millennials Really Want at Work," notes that, "Millennials value autonomy: they want to be given an assignment and then be trusted to complete it correctly."

A story in *Fast Company* from June 2015, "What Millennial Employees Really Want," reports that, "More than 50% of Millennials say they would take a pay cut to find work that matches their values."

Connect the dots between these stories, and it appears that Millennials prioritize autonomy over salary. This is because over half of Millennials, according to the *Fast Company* story, prefer work that matches their values over work that pays higher wages.

These stories are bolstered in part by my own experiences as an employer with Millennial employees. Time and again, as I've hired these employees, I've seen that their focus is on the level of autonomy at the job and the overall culture of the company.

With that reality, I've found myself having to answer, directly or indirectly, a rather unexpected question:

"What can you offer to make me want to be here?"

Not every Millennial interviewee asks me this in such blunt terms. But I can sense it in what they do ask me. It's evident as well in the way they look around my office when walking through it and during interviews. Their eyes and their words seem to flow, like tributaries, back to a question that's as fluid as the ocean...

"What can you offer to make me want to be here?"

What can I offer? What can you, as an employer, offer?

How about a company culture that recognizes autonomy and other Millennial values?

To the average Millennial employee, that's an offer they can't refuse. It speaks to their desire for happiness and personal fulfillment on the job.

Satisfy that desire and hiring Millennial employees becomes considerably easier. In addition, you're likely to have a much easier time retaining the Millennials you do hire. They'll stay at your company, pouring their best efforts into the work until...

Until...?

Until—in all likelihood—a long, long, time has passed.

Want employees who are that devoted to your company? Then you need to acknowledge the importance of company culture, particularly in the eyes of Millennials.

Neglecting culture is therefore not an option. By now, you probably get that. Still, in case it isn't clear, let me frame culture for you in a way that further drives home its importance.

Company culture is the wage of the future. It's what your employees will see as their reward and payment for working for you.

Are you up to the challenge?

Because it is a challenge. Make no mistake about that. Providing the right culture to attract and retain your employees can be downright difficult.

The difficulty is in the fact that culture is largely an abstract thing. It's difficult, if not impossible, to tangibly measure. Plus, each company's culture is bound to be unique.

Seeing this difficulty, it's easy to feel overwhelmed. Easier still to try and get by with Band-Aids, those things that provide quick fixes, rather than lasting solutions.

As employers, our most immediate Band-Aid is money. We often believe, mistakenly, that money can motivate our employees and then keep them motivated. Sadly, this just isn't the case. We can throw money at our employees with pay raises, bonuses, and other means of compensation, yet we're fighting a losing battle.

That's because the newness and excitement of the money will eventually wear off. Our employees will get over how great it is to have more money. They'll enjoy having the money all right, but the money won't have the same magnetic pull. In fact, the money may begin to feel more like a chain. Or a pair of golden handcuffs, as the expression goes.

Golden handcuffs may be golden, but they're still handcuffs, restraining our employees and keeping them from leaving a job where they feel unfulfilled.

In place of golden handcuffs and other Band-Aids, we need to use culture to attract and retain our employees. Yet the challenge, as we said earlier, is how to do that.

How, exactly, do you deal with this seemingly intangible and vague thing called culture?

A challenging question like that is bound to have an equally challenging answer. The answer in this case is environment. Environment is the key to culture.

OK, but what does environment mean?

Not much initially. In fact, it seems like we've moved backward in trying to clarify what culture is. We seem to have backpedaled away from clarity and into a new equally obscure area with the word environment.

On its own, environment is indeed too vague. So we can't stop there. We must keep going and drill down into the term environment.

Our goal is an understanding of what this term is based on.

This understanding depends on how deep we wish to drill.

If we drill down about halfway, we'll find a number of tangible things that seem to constitute environment.

One of those things would be flextime. Flextime is a condition in the workplace where there's no fixed number of vacation days. Instead, employees are free to take whatever time off they need, as long as their performance on the job doesn't suffer. Assuming they're performing and on the ball, employees can freely take vacation days and also, in some companies, work from home.

Sounds great, doesn't it? My employees certainly think so. They love flextime and consistently rank it as one of their favorite things about the company.

Your own employees may feel differently. Yet I'd wager that the majority of them would also be in favor of flextime. Flextime seems to fit with Millennials' desire for autonomy and older generations' desire for more control over their lives.

Apart from flextime, another tangible thing that's part of environment is attention to the small stuff. I'm talking about things so small, they probably seem like common courtesy. An example would be surprising an employee with a cake on her birthday.

"Who does that?"

You should.

Nonetheless, the number of companies who don't surprise their employees with a cake is far greater. Some of these companies are so large that they have no excuse. Those would be the companies that are big enough to have a Human Resources department. Somehow, though, HR departments at many such companies overlook birthday cakes and the other small things. To each his own, but it's beyond me how a big company — one with an HR department no less — can neglect such things when they make such a big difference to employees.

I have an easier time seeing how small stuff can get neglected at a small company. Chances are you can see it too.

Look at small companies, and you'll often find a situation that's as intense as the opening scene from the film *Saving Private Ryan*. No gunfire or Nazis, but the same frenzied, desperate spirit.

Like the soldiers in the film, the leaders of your average small company are also fighting against what often seems like insurmountable odds. And unlike Private Ryan, a small company's leaders don't have anyone coming to save them.

Is it any wonder then, that the small things can get overlooked, accidentally or purposely, at a small company? Survival just seems more important. Far, far more important than a birthday cake and similar concerns.

The irony, however, is that a small company may not survive long-term if it neglects too many of the small things. Attention to small things is a piece that seems to help form the overall work environment. Flextime is another of those pieces, as we've said, and there are plenty more pieces too.

Fortunately, we don't have to get into discussing all of those additional pieces that constitute environment. I can spare you pages upon pages of reading by digging even deeper.

Let's go beyond those initial tangible things and discuss the bedrock foundation of environment.

If you really want to understand what environment means as a contributor to a company's culture, then pay close attention.

Environment, at its core, is more than any of the tangible things we discussed (flextime, attention to the small things, etc.). It ultimately comes down to a single idea.

Environment is not about physical place, but about time.

Mind blown?

Let me explain.

Time consists of all of the in-between times when work isn't getting done. Those in-between times are what make an environment fun versus dull. Or exciting and worth going to each day, as opposed to boring and worth finding a reason to stay home from.

As an analogy, think back to your days in school. When you were a student in high school or even in elementary school, what made going to school fun? Was it the classroom lectures? Or was it the time between classes?

Most likely, you'll remember that in-between time as when you had the most fun. Time, for example, in high school when you hung out in the hallways, chatting with friends before the next bell rang. Or in elementary school, when you were out at recess with others on the playground.

The in-between off-times were probably what made you like going to school. If so, they formed the highlights of your school days and created a culture for you at school.

The workplace is no different. There, those off-times are just as important. The playground and the school hallways have simply been replaced by workplace staples like the water cooler and the lunchroom. These new places are where culture is being created. People think the water cooler and hallways are where this happens, but it's really the time spent that matters in terms of creating culture. It can happen anywhere.

I realize in mentioning the water cooler that this may sound like loafing around. The water cooler, after all, does tend to have negative connotations. It's often thought of as a productivity graveyard where productive employees go to "die." But there's still something to be said for the water cooler and similar scenes at work. Wherever employees congregate, that's the site where culture is being created.

You as an employer should recognize that. Recognize as well that it's part of the give and take between employer and employees. Your gut inclination, mine too, might be to oppose idle talk at the water cooler and anything else that seems like wasting time. After all, you don't want employees hanging around talking about a football game all day.

Yet you need to create balance. Your employees need to feel like they belong. Like they're united in a shared understanding and experience. As though they're members of — and I'm cringing as I write this — a tribe.

A tribe?

Yes, I know this sounds all New Age. Nonetheless, tribe is still an accurate way of describing the sense of attachment and shared bonding that employees have in the best workplace scenarios.

Allow your employees to bond like this and the results will astound you. You'll have a culture within your company that people enjoy and look forward to on Monday mornings, a company where the employees say, "Thank God it's Monday," and they will happily work there for less money.

A pipe dream?

Yes and no.

Yes, if you expect it to happen overnight. You can't just read this book and expect to snap your fingers and magically have a culture as vibrant as what I've just described.

But it's not a pipe dream in terms of it being possible in time.

And that goes for any company, regardless of its size.

So please don't tell me you're too small. You may be small, but there's no reason you can't have an incredible company culture.

I don't want to regurgitate my whole culture is important spiel. All I'll say is that small companies don't get a free pass on culture.

In fact, it's probably even more important for you, as the head of a small company, to focus on your company culture, reason being that if it's you and one employee, then your personality as the owner is the entire company's personality and thus its culture. So you can't help but be aware of the culture on that level. And it only becomes more important as you grow the company in size and assume responsibility for greater numbers of employees.

Another point about culture at the small company level is that you need to slow down and embrace small talk. I'm not saying you need to become an idle windbag who hangs out in the office lunchroom all day. What I am saying is that you can't just be no-nonsense and all-business, 24/7, when you have employees. I've seen and coached too many business owners who try that approach and inevitably fail. Heck, I myself have struggled with it too.

In my case, I'm not a jerk (at least I hope not!), but sometimes I forget to leave business owner mode and enter how was your weekend mode. In other words, I can be so focused on business affairs that I forget to make small talk with my employees about their weekend and other daily affairs that are important to them.

Whenever this happens, I have to remind myself to slow down and do the small talk, build rapport and remember once again that sometimes you can't just cut to the chase. Sometimes you have to walk at a slower pace than you'd like, engaging with small talk and other pleasantries.

"Oh, so you're being fake?"

No, not really.

You might think so as a reader, and I'll agree it could sound that way. But deep down, having reflected on this, I don't actually think it's being fake.

It's more like I have to toggle and shift to my fun side, a side of me that sometimes gets trampled by the relentless business owner side of my personality.

It's really no different than, for example, an attorney who needs to switch off attorney mode when she comes home. Or the defensive lineman who needs to stop looking for obstacles to crash into and turn off that mode when he's off the field.

The attorney, the defensive lineman, you, and I all need to temper the side of us that wants to get things done with the side of us that's a caring human being sympathetic to the wishes and concerns of others.

Wow, that sounds really touchy-feely, enough that we should probably move on. Otherwise, this is going to get pretty weird.

So let's talk about five specific things that influence your company's culture. These five influencers will further your understanding of how culture is shaped beyond our earlier points about flextime, small things, and in-between time. The five influencers of culture are:

1. Financial security

2. Attitudes and values of leadership

3. Conflict resolution

4. Communication and transparency

5. Support

Let's take a look at each of these and how they create and maintain a company's culture.

1. Financial Security

The first of our five influencers is financial security. Financial security means that your employees earn enough from your company to cover their basic needs.

Whether your employees actually spend what they earn on those basic needs is another story, a story they get to write for themselves.

On financial security: I'm not suggesting you have some socialist obligation to pay your employees' living expenses. Far from it.

My point is only that if the people who work for you — assuming they're responsible — can't cover their basic expenses, then they won't want to work for you.

You can't blame them, really. Who, for example, would come to work happy when the job didn't pay enough to cover their heating bill?

You and I both know the answer. No one would. Any employees in that position would probably drag themselves to work each day, resenting every minute on the job and fearing what their financial future holds.

That's not exactly a recipe for a healthy company culture.

Again, I'm not going to tell you how to pay your employees. But just know that their financial security ranks at the top of the list when looking at what influences company culture.

2. Attitudes and Values of Leadership

Next on that list are the attitudes and values of the company's leadership. This relates to our discussion previously about how the company's leaders define the culture through their personalities. We devoted considerable time to discussing that before, so you already know the essence of this second cultural influencer.

3. Conflict Resolution

What we haven't covered, though, is number three on the list: conflict resolution.

Conflict resolution is an area that I've gradually wised up to. I'm no longer unaware or barely conscious of this thing called conflict resolution and its role in the workplace dynamic.

What, exactly, is conflict resolution?

I'd define it as the way in which you, the employer, resolve conflicts. When one of your employees has a conflict — with you or someone else at the company — how do you set about resolving that conflict?

Is your idea of conflict resolution to tell the employee to deal with it?

Or do you take a different approach when resolving conflicts? Do you choose instead to make sure an employee in conflict gets the help he needs and feels like he's heard?

The way you resolve conflicts in this hypothetical example and elsewhere will inevitably shape the culture of your company. Conflict resolution has a kind of ripple effect that extends throughout the ranks of any company.

That's something I learned the hard way.

The lesson was cemented in my mind by that toxic employee I talked about in the last chapter, the one who did immeasurable damage to my company.

Long before she quit the company, this toxic employee was already known as a troublemaker. Her lying and manipulative ways brought her into conflict with my other employees.

I didn't see most of the conflicts happen. But I certainly heard about them. Nearly all of my employees were continually coming to me to complain about this woman and the conflicts they'd had with her.

I heard it all. And you know what my response was?

Inaction.

Yes, inaction. Even as these conflicts raged like wildfires, scorching those at my company.

My response was akin to a 911 operator who tells a caller requesting an ambulance to suck it up.

Imagine that for a moment. Picture having a severe life-threatening injury to the point where you can't walk and you're going into shock. Amidst the trauma, you somehow manage to dial 911. Then the voice on the other end tells you to suck it up. Or perhaps the 911 operator says, "Yeah, I'll handle it," and then doesn't send the ambulance.

Insane, right? Except that's how it went. Like the 911 operator in that example, I essentially told my employees the same things: "Suck it up!" and "I'll handle it." And then I did nothing, thinking the conflicts would resolve themselves with time.

Besides, this toxic employee was absolutely crushing it on the job. I loved the work she was doing and didn't want to risk disrupting her efforts.

Wow, it hurts just thinking about that now. Writing about it here in this chapter. Hindsight may be 20/20, but it doesn't excuse my inaction.

Still, I've learned my lesson. Never again will I ignore my employees and the conflicts they have. I hope you do the same. It's too important.

Here's another example as well, albeit less extreme, of why conflict resolution is so important in building a healthy company culture.

This time, the conflict occurred between me and one of my employees. We came into conflict over a problem with the sale of one our properties. With this particular property, the sale had gone sideways (i.e. bad).

My initial reaction to the problem was frustration. I grew frustrated and told one of my employees. In my mind, this employee was at fault and I needed to tell her.

In reality, though, I'd misinterpreted who was at fault. Worse yet, I came on too strong in expressing my frustration to the wrong employee.

Granted, I didn't yell at this employee who seemed in my mind to be responsible. All I said was, "This isn't working, and we need to fix it now." But delivery is everything, and I delivered these words far more abruptly than what the situation called for.

Hearing my response, the employee I spoke to didn't say anything noteworthy. We then moved on into other matters and the conflict seemed to be resolved.

Only it wasn't. Not in that employee's mind.

To her, the conflict was still alive and well, lodged in her mind and causing her tremendous discomfort, like a mental splinter.

Eventually, this employee gave me a call a few hours later.

"Hi, Mike speaking."

"Listen, I didn't do anything wrong, but you seemed upset with me."

And so we talked, this employee and me. We discussed our conflict on the phone, and the next day too, at a face-to-face meeting.

In that meeting, I ended up apologizing, telling her it wasn't her fault.

My apology — a genuine one at that — gave this employee a sense of closure. Additionally, the fact that we'd had a meeting allowed the employee to feel that her voice had been heard. We were then able to truly move on, as opposed to brushing the incident aside and letting it fester.

The takeaway for you from this example is to go the extra mile in resolving conflicts at work, any conflicts, especially the seemingly insignificant ones. It's the extra resolution that can make all the difference. Let your employees have their say, as I did, and give them the sense of closure that they need with conflicts. If you can do these things, your company's culture will grow stronger during conflicts rather than weaker.

4. Communication and Transparency

After conflict resolution, on our list of culture influencers is number four: communication and transparency. The idea here is to communicate the goals, vision, and core values of your company to all your employees. Communicate the goals/vision/core values and, in doing so, be as transparent as you can.

This is not the time to be secretive, at least where your company's goals and vision are concerned. Those things need to be on display for all to see.

Depending on your age, however, all this talk of communication and transparency could sound foreign to you. You're certainly not alone, if that's how you see it. Secrecy has long been the norm for many employers. Such employers have been extremely reluctant to tell their employees sensitive information like the company finances, core values, and strategic objectives. That kind of information has traditionally been kept as a closely-guarded secret by company brass.

In your case, you may feel inclined to be just as secretive. If that's your inclination, I'd encourage you to resist and try to be transparent. You don't have to share every single thing about your company with your employees. But you do have to open up—in all likelihood, more than you are now—about what your company stands for and where you're going.

Take your cue from me about this. The best meeting I had last year, according to my employees, was one in which we discussed our company's goals and values. At this meeting, we also got into integrity and creating a win-win for our customers.

Interestingly, none of what we discussed at this meeting involved data. Despite being fully transparent with my employees, I didn't need to give them spreadsheets, for example, or financial statements. There was no need for data, since everything we talked about was philosophical.

No data, yet full transparency and clear communication nonetheless, all of which resulted in our most popular meeting, the one employees seemed to unanimously feel was the best.

Hmm. Sounds like there's something to be said for communication and transparency. Sounds like when recognized, these two elements can electrify your employees and strengthen your company's culture too.

And they can. You'll see it for yourself too, when you focus on communication and transparency together as the fourth influencer of company culture.

5. Support

The fifth influencer of culture can be described as support. Support is the extent to which a company's leadership challenges employees and gives them the resources and freedom to succeed.

How do you know if your company, and you as its leader, truly provide employees with support? Just look at how you interact with employees when having them work on tasks.

Do you give them a task, perhaps one that requires them to stretch, and then fully support your employees in completing the task? Do you provide your employees with the necessary resources and freedom so they can win? If you do, you're being supportive of your employees, very much so.

On the other hand, if you're not being so supportive, you should work to remedy the situation. Take it upon yourself to get better at giving support and also better at recognizing its importance.

I can help you with that right now by explaining why support matters. Support leads to a culture where employees feel fulfilled. This sense of fulfillment comes from employees taking pride in their work and enjoying the sense of completing it.

The alternative is a company culture that feels like a chain gang. Ever been at a company like that? I have, and it's awful.

In those kinds of companies, support by our definition is virtually nonexistent. Instead, you the employee are given a specific objective to complete with no room to deviate in completion of said objective. Naturally, you don't feel any sense of pride or fulfillment. Neither do your fellow employees. They just feel, as you do, that the job is something to suffer through rather than something they look forward to doing.

Support sounds great, as do its comrades, freedom and resources. Yet this is all kind of vague, right?

Sure, and I get that. So let's define what these three terms mean.

Freedom means that as an employer, you're not standing over your employees, barking out orders while they try to work. You take a different approach, giving employees the freedom to complete their work.

The downside of this freedom is that your employees are going to make mistakes. No question about that. But employees have to be free to make mistakes in order for them to learn and improve.

Mistakes, therefore, are valuable. I hope you get that. If you do, you'll avoid a trap that many of us entrepreneurs fall into. We get caught up in the fear of letting go and giving our employees freedom. The fear paralyzes us, so we're unable to go all the way and grant employees the freedom to do their job.

When this happens, we must do as a famous self-help book recommends. We must "feel the fear and do it anyway," letting go and allowing our employees the necessary freedom.

While we're at it, we also need to provide employees with the resources necessary to be successful. Those resources are whatever an employee needs to get the work done.

The necessary resources are bound to vary depending on the task and your company. Examples might include a laptop, a cell phone, or maybe even a company car.

Your employees may need all of the above, some of the above, or none of the above. What qualifies as necessary resources depends on whatever is required for success out in the field.

As for support, the last of the three terms, we can define it as unconditional love. Support means that you stand by your employees, even when you give them freedom and they fail. This kind of support is essential so employees feel free to do their best. Employees can work in earnest because they know that failure on the job — within reason — will not bring them pain and anguish. They'll be supported should they fail and guided in learning from their mistakes.

What you're doing, supporting employees, is no different than the way parents might support their child. My own parents are a case in point.

When I was younger, I broke something in our house. It might have been a plate, a window, or something else. Can't remember, honestly. Yet I do remember the aftermath.

After breaking the item, I lied to my parents about it. But I'm a horrible liar, and my parents saw through my lie and knew I was the culprit.

Were they angry? Sure. But they forgave me.

My parents told me that in the future, I should just be truthful. No need to lie, they told me. Just tell us the truth next time you break something.

What a response by my parents. It certainly wasn't what I expected at that young age. Their response made an impression on me, just as a similar response will make an impression on your employees.

Your employees will inevitably "break something" while on the job, either literally breaking something or figuratively doing so in how they handle their work. When that happens, do as my parents did and be supportive. Your employees will respect you and feel more comfortable at work.

Want a workplace like that? Then you'll need to embrace the five influencers of culture:

1. Financial security

2. Attitudes and values of leadership

3. Conflict resolution

4. Communication and Transparency

5. Support

Culture.

Culture.

Culture.

It's what you're going to focus on, hopefully, in your interactions with employees at your company.

But what if you go too far in your efforts to develop culture?

What if you take this to the extreme and become a people-pleaser? Or, worse yet, turn your company into a friendly family camp where the focus is more on feelings than revenues?

Is that a risk? Of course it is...when you handle culture the wrong way.

The wrong way is to avoid key performance indicators (KPIs) and go 100% in the touchy-feely direction. Do that, and yes, you probably will have gone too far.

If, however, you have KPIs and balance those with the five cultural influencers we looked at, you'll be in much better shape. There will be little if any risk of your office becoming family camp, because cultural concerns are balanced with the results focus that KPIs bring.

KPIs, then, are really the safeguard that keeps culture from becoming so happy and loving that it cripples the company. Feelings of love and understanding toward your employees are fine, provided employees are meeting their KPIs.

When KPIs are met, then yes, be as understanding and loving as you want. It's only when the reverse is true — KPIs aren't being met — that the mood changes. Then it's time to be a little less cuddly with your employees and a lot more direct.

KPIs relate to what we said before about communication and transparency. As an employer, you'll want to be clear with your employees about how you measure their performance and communicate that metric (the KPI) with them.

You can focus on KPIs all you want, but just don't overlook one of the primary reasons employees achieve them. I'm referring now to a funny truth about KPIs. It's that employees are more likely to meet their KPIs when they feel comfortable at work, when they want to be on the job, versus feeling like they have to be there.

Comfort in this instance stems from culture. So if you create the right culture, getting your employees to hit their KPIs will be easier. This will lead to highly desirable revenues and profits for you as a company owner.

Need I say any more about culture?

Just a few more words.

Culture is there. You may not be aware of it, but it exists. The only question is whether you want to actively shape the culture to everyone's benefit, or whether you want to take your chances, do nothing, and hope that the culture works out all right on its own.

If you choose to actively shape the culture of your company, you'll need to think long-term.

Culture in this regard is like a lawn next to a driveway. The driveway is paved once and then you never have to attend to it again. But the lawn? You need to perpetually tend it, over the long-term, keeping grass from growing too high and removing any sticks or trash.

You can see thinking long-term about your company's culture as a "journey of a thousand miles." That analogy is fitting when you consider how the journey of a thousand miles begins.

It begins with a single step toward a healthy company culture. You can't stay on the sidelines, thinking it will just happen, hoping your company will magically develop a great culture without you guiding it down that path.

To help you take that first step in creating the right culture, let me tell you about what I did back when it finally clicked for me that this thing called culture was kind of a big deal.

In those days, I felt almost schizophrenic. There weren't any voices in my head or anything truly out there, but I found myself being two different people.

My friends, for example, knew me as a fun, occasionally goofy guy. My employees, in contrast, knew me to be a serious, type A, results-focused boss.

"Will the real Mike Simmons please stand up?"

Seriously, which was it? The fun goofball or the driven boss?

In truth, I was both. I still am today.

Yet I didn't feel comfortable merging my two sides. It was like how a superhero feels he can't tell anyone about his alter ego.

I wasn't a superhero by any means. But I might as well have been, with the extremes between my work and non-work personas.

In my mind, each had to be kept at a distance. My employees could not under any circumstances discover that I actually cracked jokes or laughed about dumb things. If they did, it would be as catastrophic to me and my business as terrorists getting control of a nuclear weapon. Absolute madness.

Madness? No, silliness is more like it. It's downright silly to view employee relations in those terms. Believing that a dumb joke in front of your employees will result in some doomsday scenario.

I realized this at last when I finally let both of my personalities coincide under the same roof. For better or worse, I can't remember what made it click for me. But I do remember my first step, which is what I'd promised to tell you.

The first step for me was to hire people who were a fit for both the job and my personality, all of my personality, sides A and B.

This meant I hired people who I'd want to see the next day. People who I was comfortable showing both sides of my personality to. Those were the sorts of people I began bringing in.

It sounds obvious now to take this approach when hiring employees. But like I said, it hadn't been so obvious to me before. I only grasped the truth after I'd looked back to the companies I'd enjoyed working at while an employee.

Those were the companies where I'd loved the people and the fun we'd had during those in-between times, like at lunch or around the water cooler.

Drawing on this knowledge of in-between times, my next step was to create those moments with the employees I'd hired, the ones who were a fit. To do this, I made sure there were times during the day when I interacted with these employees on a more fun, personal level.

It was a struggle at first, because I didn't want to give the wrong impression. It's easy to do that if you engage in too much fun personal pal time. The antidote is KPIs as we've seen and it's also to maintain a clear line, overall, between fun and work. Everyone you hire needs to realize that there's still a job to be done.

The inside jokes can still be funny. The football game from last night can still be worth a heated argument over. But it's all secondary to the work, which is why you and your employees are there— on the job—in the first place.

The magic happens when there's a balance. So your company is in stitches over the jokes, passionately arguing over the game, and crushing the KPIs.

Want a bit of that magic for your own company?

Then you know what to do. Take the first step, as I described, and then incorporate the other points from our discussion in this chapter on company culture.

Email me if you have any questions. I realize how difficult it can be to read a chapter—especially one as long as this—and then have to pick up the pieces. So I'm here to help you if you're lost after reading this chapter.

E-mailing me shouldn't become an excuse for not getting started. Just know that I am here, only an email away, if culture still feels as foreign to you, conceptually, as an actual foreign culture might. My email, by the way, is Mike@JustStartRealEstate.com.

After culture, before we finish this chapter, I want to address something that's sorta related. It's like the ugly stepchild of culture.

Culture gets the glowing admiration from most people, employees and employers. But this other thing — that ugly stepchild, so to speak — can't catch a break. It's the butt of countless jokes and is even met with outright hostility at times.

I'm referring to that delightful concept known as team building.

Team building.

I shudder to use the phrase because of what it often invokes in the mind's eye. Close your own eyes and picture team building. What do you see?

I see a group of out-of-shape men and women in the woods on a Saturday morning. They're all trying to scale walls and other features of an outdoor obstacle course, often quite literally jumping through hoops.

Is that team building?

Sort of. But it doesn't have to be. You can still have team building without doing it in a way that's as obvious and, in my opinion, as inane.

Team building in your company can be done with small, weekly things. It's how I approach team building at my company.

We have the money for obstacle courses, escape rooms, and all of the clichéd team building methods. But we can do just as much or more through our small weekly efforts. The most effective of those, by the way, is the money grab bucket.

What's the money grab bucket?

What's the money grab bucket? You mean you don't know?

You're obviously not one of my employees. And you definitely haven't talked with them either. For if you had, there would be no doubt in your mind as to what the money grab bucket is. No doubt whatsoever.

The money grab bucket is simply a bucket containing dollar bills of various amounts. Ones, fives, tens, and all the way up to hundreds are all in there.

The bucket's significance is that each week, some of our employees get the opportunity to draw bills from it. They get that opportunity, however, only if they've met their KPI.

Employee KPIs are tied to our company's revenue goal. Each Monday, at our weekly meeting, we ask the employees one by one to report their progress in hitting the KPIs for the previous week. Have all employees hit their numbers?

Any employees who do hit their numbers get to reach their hand into the money grab bucket. They reach in, without looking, and pull out money, money that is then theirs to keep.

Which means...

Yes, if you pull a $100 bill from the money grab bucket, it's yours to keep.

To say this creates a fun atmosphere in the office would be something of an understatement. It positively fires up my employees. Our Monday meetings are something they eagerly look forward to, and the money grab bucket fosters a level of discussion and camaraderie that's difficult to describe. It's almost like we have a mini-party on Monday mornings at the meeting. A 15-minute jam session.

Oh, and it's also great for the performance of our company. Great for our bottom line, revenues, and all that other cold hard stuff. For if an employee doesn't hit her numbers, she doesn't get to reach into the money grab bucket. So, miraculously, employees really want to make their numbers and they tend to do so.

Your company might not need a money grab bucket. But it does need some method of team building.

You can think of team building as any activities that include your whole team of employees, in a single place, and that promote a positive culture in the company. Those activities can be as simple or as complex as you want. My suggestion is to not overthink it. The reason is that with team building, a little bit tends to go a long way. My money grab bucket is an example of that.

A related analogy to the bucket would be gifts. Think about extravagant gifts you might give your kids. If you give them the gift of a single trip to Europe, will they remember that the most? Or will they remember, far more vividly and perhaps more fondly too, all the silly little stories you told them over the years?

My money's on the stories. I bet those will have a far longer shelf-life than a single, isolated act like taking the kids to Europe.

It's no different with companies. Employees will remember the small things that happen consistently, not just the grand, one-time occasions. The small, consistent things you can do for team building have the edge. They're repeatable, tend to be more meaningful, and are often more affordable.

This is why team building can work for any company, regardless of the size. It's why I'm mentioning team building to you in this book, knowing full well that you're probably not in charge of a Fortune 500 company. You might not have a company yet. But you can still do team building once you have a company with your first few employees. Keep it simple then, and do it regularly.

That's team building in a nutshell, no matter how big or small your company is. Whatever the size, your company's culture needs oxygen to stay alive. Team building is how you pump that oxygen in. With consistency in team building, you're giving company culture a steady supply of O_2, rather than coming up for a breath once a quarter.

Speaking of taking a breath, you probably need a moment to do that now. I've unloaded quite a bit on you both with team building and with culture.

Feel free to catch your breath and relax a little bit. We're at the end of this chapter, so a break certainly seems in order.

Take a break, as you see fit, and then meet me in the next chapter.

In that chapter, we'll be discussing a question that's arguably the most important one in business. It's essential, and yet few business owners give it any serious consideration.

I don't want you to make that same error, so we'll be talking about it in the next chapter. See you there!

Chapter 3 - Why?

Another chapter. And you're still here, reading along.

Why?

In other words, why are you devoting your precious time to reading this next chapter? What's in it for you?

Perhaps you're here to learn about that all-important question I mentioned at the close of the last chapter, the question that few business owners ever consider, to their detriment.

Ok, maybe that's your motivation.

But why do you want to know about this question?

"Easy," you say, "so I can use it to avoid making a big mistake in my business."

Right, but why do you want to avoid that mistake?

You: *So I can be successful in business.*

Me: *Why do you want to be successful in business?*

You: *To earn a lot of money.*

Me: *Why do you want that money?*

You: *So I'm able to travel, spend more time with my family, and not have to work nine to five.*

Me: *Why do you want to do those things?*

You: *Uh...(long pause)...so I can be independent and in control of my life?*

*

See what we just did in that imaginary dialogue above?

We began with your supposed motivation for reading this chapter. Initially, it seemed like you were motivated by the desire to learn about a question and avoid a mistake. Yet it wasn't ultimately about those things. No, with continued digging, we realized that your core motivation actually was independence and having control over your life.

If we keep digging, we might go even deeper. Is that truly your motivation for reading this chapter?

I don't know. Maybe it is, but then again, maybe not. You're the only one who knows, ultimately.

What I can tell you about your motivation — in reading or in business — is that it's probably deeper than you think. Something is compelling you to do what you do, and you ought to find out what that something is. Without understanding your motivation for reading this book, you may not finish it, or even worse, you might finish it without taking action.

How do you determine what your core motivation is?

You ask a question. That all-important one, the one I've teased you with several times now.

The question, "Why?"

Why?

Why is our topic in this chapter. Still, like in the last chapter, where culture was our topic, you have every reason to be skeptical. For if culture seemed touchy-feely and even abstract, why may seem even more so.

Yet we made it through the culture chapter, and hopefully, by the end, you understood why it is critical to your business. We managed to have a thoughtful, even-keeled discussion on culture without drowning in the quicksand of feelings and new-age fluff.

If that chapter's any indication, I know we can do it again. Right here. With this chapter on why.

To begin the discussion, let's define why.

Why is the thing that motivates you to get up in the morning, feel excited, and move into action. It's your purpose. Why is the reason you do what you do.

Like I said, this can seem fluffy. But don't let that fool you. Why remains an essential question to help you better understand yourself as you read this book and eventually start your business or grow the one you already have.

Plus, as we saw in the dialogue at the beginning of this chapter, why goes well beyond finances. Money alone doesn't work as a motivator because it simply provides a means to an end. You can see this for yourself when talking with the person in the mirror. Mention money and you'll never get her to change her ways. But tell her about the end, what the money will bring her, and that person in the mirror, namely you, will come to life.

The bottom line is that money isn't a true why, at least not for the vast majority of us. There's typically a deeper purpose that money helps us fulfill.

Why then do we treat money as though it's the ultimate motivator? We often hear that "Money makes the world go around," or "It's always about the money." My guess is that it's easier to point to money, which is very tangible, than to dig down to the intangibles.

But taking the easy road around why won't cut it long-term. If you name money as your motivator, you'll miss out on more substantial truths. Those truths would reveal your inner motives and lead you to a stronger awareness of yourself.

If you want to get better at this, at digging deeper on why, consider children and their approach. A child would probably be disappointed by the dialogue at the start of this chapter. He'd be disappointed that the stream of whys in that dialogue didn't get even more concrete or specific.

Kids are like that. They don't take the question why lightly. No, when a child asks "Why," he does so with the firm intention of finding out. He's going to get to the bottom of it or die trying.

I say die trying because, as any parent knows, a child asking why over and over again can make you want to strangle them. Maddening as it may be, most of us parents eventually find ourselves laughing at the steadfastness of our child repeatedly asking why.

Assuming we're not deranged enough to actually strangle them, it's admirable to see children persist in asking why. They seem to possess something we adults have lost over the years.

How can we overcome our laziness, to become as inquisitive about why as our children?

Step one is to define why. We've just done that, exploring what why actually means, opening your eyes to why and the reasons it's important.

Step two is recognizing that why changes over time. This means you're not set for life once you identify your why. Rather, you can expect to have different versions of why at different points in your life.

Your why at age eighteen, for example, was or is different than your why in later years, when you may be married with children. Why changes to reflect changing priorities and life events.

What if, though, you are the exception? What if your why doesn't change over time? It could be that your why is too broad. Wanting, for example, to be a good person is unlikely to change. It's also unlikely to make you spring out of bed each morning or work late into the night. "Being a good person," therefore, lacks the sort of magnetic pull a deeper why has, so the deeper one is the one we're looking for.

With all this talk about why, you may be wondering about my why as an author. I'm asking you about yours, so it's only right for me to share mine.

Before I tell you my why, let me start by saying that it's definitely changed over time. While I'm hazy about my exact why twenty years ago, I can promise you that it's not the same as today's.

My why has evolved like a business plan would over time. The business plan's evolution reflects changes in the nature of the business, as my why has changed with changes in my life.

Amidst those changes, my present why is the following:

"To create something in my life that helps make the lives of my kids and their kids easier and is also something they look upon with pride."

Notice anything unusual about my why?

Look closely and you'll see it doesn't mention business at all.

This leads to my next point, which is that your why and your business' why should not be the same. Each why needs to be separate to reflect the differing priorities and realities.

As evidence, consider now the why for my business:

"To create a win-win-win through real estate so customers can move on from the problem they're facing."

See how this why, the one for my business, says nothing about helping my kids or leaving a legacy? Those concerns are separate from my business and the different whys reflect that.

My business has its own why, much as yours will or does, because a company is its own entity. The company has its own why, and you and I each have ours. But each has only one, just one why per person or company.

Your why will not be that of your business, yet the two can intersect. You'd see this, for instance, if your personal why was making a difference in society. With that as your why, you'd see it intersect with that of your business, if the business' why was based around providing affordable housing.

Whys can certainly intersect, although it's not mandatory. What is mandatory, however, is that your business' why supports your personal why. In describing this, I'd compare your business to a person. This person, your business, has its own why, yet you created it. You, like Dr. Frankenstein, stitched together the company and gave it life. Now that your company is alive, you must live with it. If you can't, it's time to go back to the lab, for you've created the wrong person (company).

None of that matters, of course, unless you actually know your why. So how do you determine it?

The process looks similar to our opening dialogue at the start of this chapter. The dialogue was there for a reason. I wanted you to get a glimpse of what it's like to use why as a tool for uncovering deeper motivations.

From that earlier dialogue, you can see what's involved in finding your why. You begin by questioning what you want and then drill down to the heart of it, with why after why after why.

Eventually, like a drill burrowing downward, you'll reach a point where you can't go any deeper. You'll have hit a bedrock foundation, upon which further drilling proves futile. Whatever you reach last in your drilling is your why.

But what if it's money? What if you drill down and still find that money is your final why. What then?

Personally, I have a hard time accepting that. All the same, for argument's sake, let's say money is ultimately your why.

My advice to you would be to embrace it.

Don't feel weird if your why is money rather than a desire to make a difference or help people. I happen to believe that making a difference and helping others are very worthwhile pursuits. You probably do too. Nonetheless, if your core why doesn't resonate with those two things, and is instead to make a billion dollars, that's fine. You don't need to adopt a more altruistic why in line with that of celebrity entrepreneurs, online influencers, and speakers of TED talks.

Your why can be making a billion dollars.

With one notable caveat.

The caveat is that if money really is your why, deep down, it should absolutely electrify you. You should be springing out of bed in the morning, driven by the thought of money and only money.

If that's not happening, you need to reexamine your why. It's probably not money. Not any more. Whatever short-term motivation the thought of money provided, it's now gone. You'll need to return to the drawing board, as the saying goes, and reassess your why.

Once you've done so and have identified your ultimate why, you'll know. The true why will be apparent and it'll work for you. That sounds vague and I wish it were clearer. Yet your ultimate why is too personal and individualized for me to describe much more. Like a Supreme Court justice said, in a famous case involving pornography, "You know it when you see it."

That's how you'll know your why once you've dug deep and hit upon it.

Once you've reached that point, you may want to write down your why. By writing it down, you won't be at risk of forgetting it.

I don't have my why written down. Nor is it tattooed on my right arm or recorded for daily listening. None of that is necessary because I don't feel at risk of forgetting my why. My why is too important for me to forget. I'd compare it to the way most parents don't forget the date their child was born. It's just one of those things that sticks in your mind.

If you do forget, it probably wasn't that important to you, whatever it was, your child's birthday or your why.

Having said that, you can still write down your why. I encourage you to do it, because it will help you get through difficult days. The point is to know your why, with or without the written reminders.

In addition, treat your why as more of a North Star versus a GPS. Think about the two and you'll catch the difference.

A GPS needs to be watched continuously to ensure you're going the right way. Avert your eyes from the GPS and you can easily lose track of what it's telling you.

Your why, on the other hand, like the North Star, doesn't need to be monitored nearly as vigilantly. It doesn't change as rapidly as the data on the GPS. You can look away and then return to your why and the North Star without either having been lost. Both will still be there when you come back, ready to assist you in moving forward.

We've talked at length now about your personal why as well as your business' why. Yet you're not alone, are you? Not when running a business.

You have or will have employees. Since these employees are people, just like you, guess what they'll have?

Their own unique whys.

Each and every one of your employees will have a why that drives them into action. Or, more appropriately, a why that drives them to work for you each day. We're not talking about self-driving cars here either. That isn't what's going to drive your employees into work. It may literally be the thing, as self-driving technology becomes more common. But the true driver of your employees is going to be a decidedly old-school question, why.

You must therefore know your employees' why. But here's the bad news. You can't ascertain it through the same means as finding your own why. That process we discussed a few pages ago, of drilling down with repeated whys, isn't going to work on your employees. Try it and they're bound to be as irritated as you are when a child starts asking why. It's interesting how we can be OK with asking ourselves a stream of whys internally, yet we get irritated when questioned like this by others.

Interesting, yet true. So we must face the facts and adjust our strategy.

In place of the perpetual why, we need a more nuanced approach, one resembling that of a detective. It's a better model when uncovering your employees' whys.

As a detective, you look for clues. Some of these clues can be found in what your employees choose to talk about on a regular basis. An employee, for example, who's always talking about his wife and kids is making it clear what he finds important. This employee's wife and kids are evidently something he values tremendously.

Another example would be an employee who's constantly talking about missing her daughter's events. In this latter case, you can glean two things from the employee's words.

First, it'll be apparent to you that this employee finds her daughter important. Then, from the frequent talk about missing their daughter's events, you'll also realize that this employee values free time. Armed with these two pieces of knowledge, you'll be better able to support and motivate this particular employee in the future.

Nonetheless, even with all this talk of being a detective, you can still ask questions. I'm not issuing a gag order forbidding you from asking your employees about their why. No, there are indeed times when you can do just that and do it directly.

You may not even mention the word why in your questioning. But your questions will be closely tied to it. Here are some examples of questions you could ask to gain information about your employees' whys:

1. What makes you want to come in here each day?

2. What specifically do you want to get out of this job and this company?

3. What's important to you?

When asking these questions, I'd encourage you to come from a place of warmth and genuine interest. Make it a relaxed, enjoyable conversation rather than a police interrogation.

Amidst such conversations, make sure you're being an active listener. If you have difficulty listening and want to talk instead, just remember the ratio of mouths to ears. As humans, we have only one mouth compared to two ears. Let that be a sign, a reminder that listening is more important than talking in your interactions with employees.

Once you've engaged in active listening, relaxed questioning, and detective work, you'll be able to identify the why for each of your employees. It may take you some time, but eventually you'll have a clear sense of everyone's whys.

Once you have this knowledge, it's time to put it to use.

The most important application of your employees' whys is motivation. Awareness of each employee's why allows you go beyond money to motivate your employees with things they'll care about for the long-term.

We could do that, for example, with the employee we mentioned earlier. This was the employee who wanted to be at her daughter's events. To motivate her, we could tie time off to meeting sales goals. So if this employee met her sales goals, she'd be able to take time off in the future for attending all of her daughter's events. Think that's going to motivate the employee? Absolutely, and it'll be an even deeper motivation than if we'd offered her a few hundred dollars as the reward.

The situation here is analogous to birthday gifts. Think back to your last birthday and you'll see what I mean. Assuming you received birthday presents, which ones do you remember most fondly? Generic gift cards? Or presents that were homemade and deeply personal?

I suspect it's the personal ones. Those sorts of gifts stir us on a deeper emotional level than just another generic gift card. The same applies to motivating employees. Like the gift cards, you can throw money at your employees as a motivator, or you can foster more lasting, long-term results with a motivator that's as personalized as the homemade gift. You decide, though you can probably guess which approach I'd recommend.

While we're on the topic of motivating employees, let's deal with the proverbial elephant in the room: the issue of manipulation. We need to acknowledge it since using employees' whys to motivate them can seem manipulative.

I'd argue that it isn't, not if you're trying to genuinely understand your employees to support them on the job and aid them in achieving their potential. If that's where you're coming from, then no, it's not manipulative. It's no more manipulative than a sports coach using what's important to his athletes as a positive motivator, or a teacher motivating his students to get better grades with those things the student cares about. Or even a parent, using compassion to stir her child into positive behavior. None of that is manipulative in the bad sense.

Nor is this approach, which you're welcome to model. This approach is to hold one-on-one meetings with my employees. The meetings are designed to provide me with a deeper sense of my employees' whys by chatting with them about what's working and what's not.

As you might imagine, I approach these meetings in a relaxed way. Each is a dialogue and my employees are never put on the stand, so to speak, with lawyer-like questioning. As a result, I learn the whys from those I employ, and it also deepens the personal bond I have with each of them.

Another of my approaches, which I'd humbly encourage you to steal, is to look for small ways to acknowledge your employees' whys.

In a given week — or even a given day — there are bound to be occasions when a small act on your part in support of an employee's why will go a long way.

Here's an example so you can grasp the idea better. Recall once more the employee who's always missing her daughter's events. For this employee, you might tell her on a given day that she can leave thirty minutes early to make one of her daughter's events. Letting the employee cut out a half-hour ahead of time won't have much impact on you, yet it will probably electrify the employee.

Can you see the power of this small act and others like it? Such acts cost you little to nothing, while they mean the world to your employees. So keep your eyes open for these opportunities each day. They're waiting for you, I'm sure of it.

One more point for you about employee whys. I put this particular point last because it's necessary to know, yet unpleasant too. The why for any of your employees could be downright awful. One of your employees could have a why that's based on rotten and horrifically selfish ideas.

Needless to say, this employee's why would not mesh with your why nor with your company's why. Faced with this reality, you might have to part ways with the employee. It wouldn't make sense, for instance, to have an employee with a why steeped in selfishness if your company's why was charity-oriented.

Are there exceptions to this? Sure. But just be aware of the need, in most cases, for employees' and employers' whys to align.

That last point hinted at another why. If you're paying attention, you probably saw it when I mentioned the company why.

Remember from the beginning of this chapter?

Since a company has its own why, you should know what that why is. You're the company's leader, after all, the one who's in charge of its employees. Moreover, knowledge of your company's why — what your company stands for — will be tremendously helpful when inspiring your employees.

As evidence of this point about company whys, consider an example from my own company.

At my company, we operated for many years without ever telling our employees about the company's why. It just didn't seem necessary.

One day, though, we took a chance and had a meeting to discuss the why of our company. In this meeting, my partner and I presented our company's why along with related details like company values, principles, and goals.

It's worth noting that the entire meeting was completely free of any data or hard numbers. In fact, one might even say it was one of the lightest or fluffiest meetings we've ever had.

But after the meeting, employees wanted to print out and hang up the company values and other supposedly light material we'd discussed. In their eyes, there was nothing fluffy about any of the material. Instead, they viewed it as meaningful and inspirational in guiding their work each day.

My employees' reaction to our company why makes sense when cast in the following analogy. The analogy is of driving a car. If you're the only one in the car, you know where the car's going. You also know why you're driving.

Still, that's just you, isn't it? Other people won't automatically know where the car is going nor the reason for the trip, not unless you tell them. And you'd better do that. Otherwise, you won't get many people wanting to get in the car and ride with you.

Your company is no different than the car. If employees don't know the company's why and direction, they'll be equally hesitant to get on board as employees or stay on board for the long-term.

If you need any more evidence about the importance of communicating your company's why, I recommend looking at cult leaders. Crazy as most of them are, the average cult leader also wields crazy levels of influence.

What's his secret? How is it that cult leaders get their followers to do such outlandish things? It's worth knowing if you want your employees to drink the proverbial Kool-Aid.

How do the cult leaders do it? Through the same process we've discussed: telling their followers about the cult's direction and what it stands for. These things then fill the followers with a sense of meaning, which they can attach to and be inspired by.

You probably won't go as far as the cult leaders. But their example still reinforces the need to make your company's why well-known and not a tightly-held secret.

After company whys, you may also need to consider the why of your business partner. A business partner is a person who's an equal partner with you in the business you're running. It might also be another company or organization that your business relies on to perform helpful services, like a strategic business partner. Either of these two scenarios is applicable when thinking about your business partner and his why.

In the first scenario, where the business partner is a person, his why should align with your own why. There can be some slight differences between these two whys, but the fewer the differences, the better. For if the differences are too great, then you'll essentially have two North Stars for your employees to follow.

One of those North Stars will be your own why, lighting up the night and guiding the employees onward. But then there will also be another North Star burning just as brightly. See the problem? The issue is that your employees won't know which North Star to follow.

To prevent this problem, make sure your business partner's why isn't radically different from your own. Unfortunately, I can't tell you on an individual basis exactly how radically different is too much. It's going to vary, naturally enough, depending on your situation. What I can tell you, though, is that neither your why nor your business partner's why should conflict with the company's why. Nor should the company's why conflict with your own why. Assuming those three whys are compatible, essentially forming a sort of three-legged stool, you should be fine.

My business partner is younger than me. In spite of the age difference, our whys still mesh with the why of our company. So our employees don't have the sense of there being two strikingly different North Stars.

What about the second scenario we talked about, when your business partner is a company or organization? A strategic business partner, in other words.

If that's the case, then you'll need to change the way you see why. A change is necessary since you're no longer dealing with a person who, as an equal partner, can affect your business. The partner this time is a company or organization. Its why will be related to marketing. You'll have to assess it in your particular situation, because company/organization whys vary. Nevertheless, once you do know its why, you'll have a profound advantage. This is because you'll be able to see how the strategic business partner can support your business. Plus, you'll also be able to build a strong, supportive relationship with the strategic business partner since you'll know its motivation.

Here's an example of how this works with strategic business partner whys. Suppose your strategic business partner is a company run by a person who's deeply religious.

From the get-go, the other company's leader makes it clear to you that her faith impacts all her dealings with others. Seeing that, you'd need to avoid doing things that didn't align with the leader's religion. You'd also need to understand the leader's trigger points, those things related to her religion or other views, things that make her tick.

That's a long-winded way of saying you want to respect the views held by your strategic business partner(s). Be sensitive to them.

Common sense, right? Sure, and if it somehow wasn't, then now you know.

Continuing on, there's one more why for you to keep in mind. This final why is that of the customer.

Your customers' whys are their motivation for using the products or services in your industry, the things that drive them to seek out such products or services. They also help you understand what on a broader level your customers are driven by.

Ask these questions to many business owners and they'll likely be without answers. Indeed, the average business owner tends to be clueless about the why of his customers. He hasn't the faintest idea of what's driving his customers onward.

The lack of knowledge translates into marketing efforts that don't work. A business owner may send mailings out. They may place ads in relevant publications. That's just the tip of the iceberg when it comes to all potential marketing channels that could be employed.

Yet when a business owner doesn't understand the customers' whys, none of that marketing is likely to work. Worse, a business' owners may come to feel that a given form of marketing just doesn't get results period.

Maybe that's true. Maybe. But it's far more likely that the problem lies in the business owner's lack of awareness of his customer's why.

If you want to avoid this error, don't focus on what you do in your business. Think instead about what your customers want. Know, too, who your ideal customer is.

As guidance, consider how I connect with my customers' whys. In one of my businesses, we buy residential properties from homeowners. This means we're marketing directly to homeowners. They're our ideal customers.

In reaching out to homeowners, we could simply say, "We want to buy your house." That's what we as a company want to do. It's the ultimate goal of our marketing. But it's not our customer's goal. Nor is it what the customer wants. Our marketing therefore can't just be about wanting to buy the customer's house. We must enter the customers' world and tailor our marketing to what they find important. This results in marketing which asks customers, "Do you need to sell your home?" We also, where possible, dig even deeper in speaking to customer whys.

We'll ask in our marketing, "Have you inherited a home you don't want?" Many of our customers are in that position, and our marketing thus speaks perfectly to their needs and situation.

Your own marketing will ideally go deep into the customer's why. Still, you can't ultimately know deep down what your customer's why is. You'd have to be psychic to know that. And let's face it, none of us are, not even those psychics you can call on the Psychic Hotline.

Since we can't read minds, the next best thing is to think about our customers as a collective group. What is it that they collectively want? Answer this and you'll be on track to identifying your customer's why.

That ends our discussion of why. Drawing this chapter to a close, let's turn our attention to the next core concept: partnering.

If you're wondering whether to partner in starting or expanding your business, you'll enjoy the upcoming chapter. Having partnered in my own business, I've got a wealth of insights for you on the topic. Join me on the next page, and we can jump right in.

Chapter 4 - Partnering

You know this is going to be hard, right?

I just want to make sure of that. Somehow it slipped my mind when we were getting acquainted way back in the introduction.

Back then, I was focused on demolishing any idea you might have about why you can't just start. That focus, though, may have blinded me to something equally important.

In discussing Just Start, I never talked to you about the difficulties you'll face when you take action.

Why mention those difficulties? Won't it kill the buzz I'm trying to create? No. Not any more than knowing your parachute might not open when skydiving. That knowledge may scare the hell out of you. But it's knowledge you need to have. And once you do jump, it won't diminish the adrenaline rush you'll get from skydiving.

Same goes here with the difficulties you'll face when you Just Start. The adrenaline's still going to be pumping through your veins, regardless of how hard it is.

Ok, but why mention those difficulties now? At this point in the book?

Why? Because those difficulties tie in to this chapter's topic. This chapter, if you'll recall, is about partnering.

As we begin the discussion, I want to make sure you're aware of an underlying force that often pushes business owners into partnering.

Understand that this underlying force begins with knowing that once you're in business, it's going to be hard. Like, really, really hard.

Starting? That's the easy part. The difficult part is staying in the game over the weeks, months, and years that follow.

And you know what makes it so difficult?

There are a lot of reasons. But let me give you the biggest one. It's one word. A word that, in itself, strikes fear in the hearts of many entrepreneurs. A word that you'll never hear on any entrepreneurship talks, podcasts, or YouTube videos.

That word is loneliness.

Loneliness brings business owners to their knees. It makes grown people cry. And when the pain and anguish from it become too great, loneliness leads these distraught entrepreneurs to do the unthinkable. They commit one of the cardinal sins of owning a business.

They partner for companionship rather than for growth. In other words, these entrepreneurs partner up so they won't be alone. If having a partner leads to growth, then all the better. But growth is not the driving reason behind the partnership in these cases.

You won't fall victim to that, though, will you? I mean, you're tough, right? Maybe you do crossfit or martial arts, and that proves it. Or you know by some other means that you're tough. Tough enough to stand strong. So tough that you won't crack and go running for a shoulder to cry on, the shoulder, in this case, of a business partner.

Far be it for me to judge your toughness. I'll give you the benefit of the doubt. You probably are one bad mofo. Trouble is, this is the worst possible time to prove it. We're in peacetime right now. The heavy — and I do mean *heavy* — artillery of loneliness hasn't begun to pound you yet. You're not yet running up Omaha Beach on D-Day under the enemy shelling.

When the artillery barrage does begin, I want you to be prepared. This chapter will help you. Over the next dozen or so pages, I'm going to provide you with my best advice on overcoming entrepreneurial loneliness. That advice will be part of the discussion in this chapter on partnering.

Just to be clear, this chapter is not all about loneliness as an entrepreneur. Instead, the chapter is about partnering, and we'll be talking about loneliness too, since it often causes entrepreneurs to partner when they shouldn't.

Let's begin the discussion now with what I believe is the truth about partnering. Having built a seven-figure business and coached countless entrepreneurs, I now believe that partnering is largely unnecessary. Quite often, you really don't need a partner. You can get by on your own, managing your company and its employees all by yourself.

I'd even go so far as to say that for every 10 people who think they need to partner, only about one or two really do. That means only about 10-20% of business owners benefit from partnering.

The stats above are based only on my experiences, and I could certainly be wrong. But even if I am and the stats are higher — like 50% — it would still mean that a lot of entrepreneurs don't really need to partner.

Why then does everyone think partnering is necessary?

We've covered one of the reasons: loneliness.

Another would be the sense of overwhelm at everything you need to do to run a business. In this situation, you probably just need help with your business. And you can get help without having a partner.

As an example, think about a toy store in December during holiday season. With the holidays approaching, this toy store is continually packed with shoppers. The store's owner is stressed out as she struggles to keep up with the surge of shoppers. Despite having four employees, the owner still feels overwhelmed.

What should the owner of the toy store do?

She should do what countless other stores do during times of overwhelm: hire more employees.

The new employees can be brought on as seasonal help or for the long-term. But either way, having them is bound to reduce the toy store owner's sense of overwhelm.

Hiring makes far more sense than another supposed solution. The other solution is partnering. But the store owner would have to be crazy to partner in this situation. It would be nothing less than insanity for her to permanently give up half of her ownership in the company to a business partner just to have less stress during a busy season. Hiring would accomplish the same result, less stress, without reducing her share of ownership in her company.

The takeaway from this example is that needing help in your business is not the same as needing a partner. Make sure you're able to differentiate between the two. Don't confuse partner with helper or assistant.

To eliminate confusion, let's define what it means to partner. Partnering is generally defined as bringing someone into your business as an equal owner, so that each of you own 50% of the business.

In my business, I have a partner who handles the sales side. In exchange for handling sales, my partner gets to own 50% of the company.

Hearing about my business partner, you might be confused. After all, I've just spent the last few paragraphs arguing against partnerships. Why, then, would I have ever gotten a business partner? Seems like a contradiction, doesn't it?

Was loneliness the underlying reason why I chose to partner?

No. I can say honestly it wasn't loneliness. You don't have to take my word for it either. If you were to ask my friends and my wife, they'd tell you the same thing. So would the baristas at the Starbucks near my house. None of them would be able to tell you about my business. Nor would they know me by name.

What I'm getting at is that I was never that entrepreneur who was overwhelmed by loneliness, talking the ears off of the baristas at Starbucks or the restaurant staff when eating out. You know, the entrepreneur who thinks that servers want to hear all about his business in-depth, that the wait staff somehow cares about this entrepreneur's third quarter initiatives or what so-and-so said on a recent conference call.

So if it wasn't loneliness, then why did I partner?

Looking back, I'd say my decision was driven by two main factors. The first was that my partner complimented my strengths in business. He brought a level of skill and competence in the area of sales, which I lack. I'm not terrible at selling. But if you compared me to my business partner, it's not even close. My business partner is the salesperson's salesperson, the kind who can sell snow in the winter or get a vegan to buy a steak. He's good, damned good at sales. So good that it contributed to my decision to partner with him.

The other reason for that decision was my awareness of three distinct benefits that come from partnering. These benefits are the following:

Benefit #1: Having a True Sounding Board

When you partner with the right person, that individual becomes a true sounding board for you. You can bounce ideas off him with confidence, knowing your partner isn't just humoring you. Instead, he's listening and engaged because he has the same level of interest in the company's success as you do. Your partner is therefore a sounding board in the truest sense. And that's priceless.

What makes your partner so receptive and interested? It's simple. He has just as much to lose or gain from the business as you do.

Remember when I told you a few chapters ago that your employees will never care as much as you? This is different. You're not dealing with employees anymore. You're dealing with an individual who's as invested — financially and emotionally — in the company's success as you are.

This individual, your partner, isn't just collecting a paycheck like your employees. No, your partner is doing a whole lot more. She's aiding you in managing the company and setting its direction. Your partner also has skin in the game through her ownership stake in the company and perhaps money she invested in the company too. With skin in the game, your partner can't help but care and be as interested as you are.

Benefit #2: Freedom to Take Time Off

Partner with a person who cares as much about the business as you do, and you gain the freedom to take time off. You can step away from your business with the confidence that things will run smoothly while you're gone. The business will keep calm and carry on because it's being managed by a partner who has the same goals and interest in the company as you. So while you may be off on vacation somewhere, the business will continue to run as if you were still around overseeing it.

Being able to step away from your business like this is huge. Surprisingly, though, not too many business owners ever consider partnering for this reason. They never think about how having a partner — the right partner — will allow them to take time off.

That's a shame, because time off is a requirement for success in business. You need to be able to get away. Your getaway could be a week's vacation. Or it might be something shorter and simpler. Maybe you just take a day to unplug, have a relaxed lunch with the spouse, and remember that there is life outside of your business.

Wait, there's life outside of business? Seriously?

Yeah, I realize it seems unbelievable. It runs counter to the go-go-go image of the entrepreneur. That image portrays the entrepreneur as a relentless workaholic, the kind of person who works and works and works. The kind of person who is always at work.

Now for the record, there is nothing wrong with workaholism. There is also nothing wrong with hustling in the sense of legally pushing to grow your legitimate business.

Both of these behaviors are tremendously important for business owners. You probably know that already. But I have to mention it anyway because there are certain books out there that condemn excessive levels of work.

Frankly, who's to say what excessive is? But even if it can be defined, there's still no way around seemingly excessive levels of work. It's unavoidable if you want to grow a business to stratospheric heights. I know this from my own experiences growing a multi-million dollar business from scratch. And I'm hardly the first person to point out the importance of hard work. That idea is as old as our country.

Look back at the founding of the United States, and you'll see that many of the founders were Protestant. This faith stresses hard work, with sayings like, "Idle hands are the devil's playthings," and the so-called Protestant work ethic. Is it any wonder that we as Americans are such believers in hard work? No matter what faith we come from, we still share the founders' belief that it's good to work your butt off.

When this belief is applied to business, the result is the image of the entrepreneur as that go-go-go person. That's what we're supposed to shoot for, the 80-hour workweek and sleeping on our office floor.

If we reject that idea, the media and other entrepreneurs will push back. On YouTube, for example, you'll find videos about hard work posted by social media icon Gary Vaynerchuk, aka Gary Vee. Some of these videos are stinging in their criticism of laziness and people who don't go-go-go every minute of every day. Watch any of them and you'll probably feel revved up. Ready to kick ass and take names. And ready to work harder than you've ever worked before.

There's just one problem. Not with Gary's videos, or others like them; those are fine. The problem is that the fire of motivation, the one which blazes in you after watching an inspiring video or even reading this book, won't burn forever. It's not like that flame they keep lit in Washington D.C., the flame that burns at John F. Kennedy's grave.

Unlike the flame at JFK's grave, you don't have anyone standing by to keep your entrepreneurial fire from burning out. It's on you to do that.

How?

Take time off.

Get away, unplug, and relax. It'll keep you from burning out as an entrepreneur over the long haul. Plus, you might actually enjoy yourself.

If you need any more reason to take time off, then look again at Gary Vee. Even this workaholic of workaholics takes breaks. In his case, Vaynerchuk took all of August 2017 off. During that time, he didn't do social media posts, speaking engagements, or business-related activities in general. Instead, Vaynerchuk completely disconnected and went on a family vacation.

Compelling isn't it? That's got to be one of the best indications that occasionally taking time off isn't wrong at all. If you've truly gone hard on your business, working relentlessly 24-7, then by all means take some time off.

Oh wait, that's right. You can't take time off, can you? I mean, you could. But then you'd come back and find your business ruined. The office would be on fire, piranhas would be swimming in the bathroom sink, and your employees would have fled with all the company's money.

Maybe, just maybe, it wouldn't be that bad. Yet surely there would be some damage to your business if you took time off. Enough damage that you can't just step away. Not when you're the only one running things.

But if you get a partner, someone to join you in running the business, then you're no longer enslaved. You can take time off.

While partnering helps you get away from your business, I realize that it's not the only way. In other words, I understand that in this four-hour work-week world, there are various hacks that can help you replace yourself. Those hacks can in certain cases help you get away despite not having a business partner. They are, however, the exception to the rule.

In addition, it often takes a long time to replace yourself using hacks (i.e. outsourcing, systems, etc.). That's assuming that these hacks work. You might easily spin your wheels and get nowhere.

In place of all that hacking and cleverness, why not just get a business partner? You'll achieve the same result (time off) and you won't have to build a complicated system of apps, virtual assistants, and written SOPs (standard operating procedures).

Benefit #3: Exponential Increases in Your Business' Potential

This third benefit of a partnership is that when done correctly, a partnership can increase your business' potential exponentially. An exponential increase happens because you're not just cloning yourself.

Clone yourself and you get someone who's got identical business skills. That doesn't accomplish anything. You're no better off because all you've done is amplify your weaknesses. Whatever your weaknesses were, you've simply enhanced them by bringing on another person (your clone) who shares these same weaknesses. It's like you've taken two steps forward just as your weaknesses have taken you two steps backward.

You want to avoid that. The way to do it is by seeking a business partner who's great at the things you're terrible at, the sort of partner who's more of what you're not.

When you find a partner like that, you change the math in your business. The equation of one plus one no longer equals two. Instead, one plus can equal three, four, five, or more.

As a brief example, think again about Apple. Can you imagine what the one plus one of Jobs and Woz's partnership was? Their partnership's one plus one probably equaled 1,000 or more.

Even if you and your partner's one plus one doesn't equal 1,000, it's still going to be more than two. That's practically inevitable if you've got the right business partner. And when you do, your business's potential can grow exponentially.

*

Seeing the three benefits we've just covered, you might be thinking now of partnering. If you are, then I'd encourage you to give it some honest thought. Do a bit of soul-searching to see why exactly you're interested in partnering. Are you purely interested in reaping the benefits of partnering? Or could your interest be driven instead by loneliness and/or a sense of overwhelm?

Only you know the answer, and I'm not here to judge you. I will say, though, that if you find yourself wanting to partner as an escape from loneliness or overwhelm, then don't do it. You don't need to give up half of your company just to have someone to talk to or an extra pair of hands to help out around the office. There are practical solutions to these problems that don't involve partnering. I'll be giving you a few of those solutions later on in this chapter, so stay tuned.

In the meantime, let's assume it's not loneliness or overwhelm that's driving you. Let's say you really are driven by a desire to benefit from a partnership in the ways described here. You're thinking specifically about how you plus your partner (one plus one) can, for example, equal 40. Or you're looking for someone who can man the fort while you're taking time off. These are both perfectly valid reasons to think about partnering. If that's where your head's at, then keep going and take the next step.

The next step is to see whether a potential business partner meets four requirements. These four requirements are like checkboxes. You must be able to check all of them off when considering your potential partner's background. If you can't, then the partnership probably won't work.

As an analogy, what you're doing here with the checkboxes is like what goes on when you're deciding whether or not to get married. You take a careful look at the person you're considering marrying. As you do, you think about whether the person meets certain requirements.

One of those requirements could be that anyone you marry must also want kids. They may also have to be of the same religious faith as you or be a non-smoker. You get the idea. There are certain things you'll look for in the other person when considering marriage. Why then should partnering in a business be any different?

It shouldn't be. Not when partnering resembles marriage so closely.

I'm hardly the first person to make that analogy between partnering for business and marriage. It's popular because partnering is indeed like marriage, minus some really cool stuff.

You can't, for instance, give your business partner breakfast in bed. That's one of the perks of having a spouse. But it doesn't generally work out so well with a business partner.

Imagine how creepy that would be. Waking up to find that your business partner broke into your house while you were asleep. He's come in the night and set a tray of bacon and eggs or fruit and yogurt on your nightstand.

Yeah, that's creepy.

At any rate, let's walk through those four requirements. As we get going, I want to reiterate that all four must be met before you choose a partner. This isn't like a test in school, where you could get by with three of the four questions satisfied, earning a score of 75%, a C grade. All four considerations we're about to cover must be met. Otherwise, you're at risk of a business nightmare, one far scarier than an unexpected breakfast in bed.

The nightmare I'm referring to is when you realize, after building a successful business and taking on a partner, that you and your business partner aren't on the same page. You and your business partner might lack the same goals. You might also not like your partner as a person.

Under normal circumstances, you and your business partner could just go your separate ways. But that's harder now, much harder, because of the successful business you've built together. The business has grown so large and profitable that you're in for a rough time when ending the partnership. Things could turn ugly, just like a divorce following marriage.

The good news is that this nightmare is avoidable. You can avoid it by putting your potential business partner through the paces with our four requirements. They are:

1. Identical risk tolerance

2. Alignment of goals

3. Common hunger

4. Complementary skill sets

Requirement #1: Identical Risk Tolerance

For this requirement, you'll need to ask:

"Do we, my potential partner and I, have the same risk tolerance?"

This question will get you thinking about how much risk your partner is willing to take. You'll begin to consider, for example, whether they're super risk-averse. That's going to be a problem if you're super aggressive. The reverse is also true. If you happen to be the play-it-safe type and your prospective partner loves risk, then the partnership is also not going to work.

Identical risk tolerance is a must for any partnership. You can see evidence of this with me and one of my earlier business ventures. This venture involved flipping houses.

As a house flipper, I chose to partner with my wife. Given how extraordinarily talented she is, I figured my wife would be the perfect business partner. She was too, except for one thing. Just one thing and one thing only. Her risk tolerance was much, much lower than mine. Apart from this one thing, everything else was perfect. We were fully aligned on absolutely everything else, except being equally bullish on taking risks.

At the start, our differences in risk tolerance weren't a huge deal. We had some initial success. It was also unbelievably great to have my wife as a business partner. She was supportive and more than satisfied her duties as partner.

Ultimately, though, my wife and I — as business partners — hit a limit on what we could accomplish together in our house flipping venture. The limit came from our differing risk tolerances.

132

My wife, for example, was conservative with the money in our business. I, on the other hand, was ultra-aggressive, wanting to take bigger risks in order to scale our business. Our differing views put a cap on how big our business could become. It was like putting a speed governor on a racecar. The driver in the car might have a need for speed, yet his car will never hit the red line. It's just not possible. So it was with my wife and I in our house flipping business.

Thankfully, this story has a happy ending. It ended with my wife doing something that further demonstrates her intelligence and maturity. Unlike other spouses, my wife was smart enough to see the differences that existed in our risk tolerance levels. How she managed to see this while also handling the lion's share of our family responsibilities is beyond me. That takes a level of brainpower, time management, and multitasking that I'd love to have. My wife, though, has these skills, and so she was able to realize that we weren't on the same page with taking risks.

Seeing this, my wife made the decision to step away from the partnership. She did this with warmth and sincerity, giving me her blessing to keep going in the business without her.

As you might expect, this example with my wife is the exception rather than the rule. You're unlikely to have a business partner who gracefully steps aside when it's clear that your risk tolerance levels differ. That's why it's essential, at the beginning, to know whether a potential business partner does in fact meet this first of our four requirements.

Requirement #2: Alignment of Goals

Do you and your prospective partner have the same goals for the company? That question is at the core of requirement #2. If you can't answer the question with, "Hell, yeah!" then you need to pass on the prospective partner.

Passing is easy in cases where your answer is a strong no. But what about those times when your answer is sorta, meaning it looks like your potential partner has the same goals, but there might be differences too.

In times like these, it can be tempting to turn "sorta" into "yes." The temptation could come because you like the person you're considering partnering with. Or you might figure that having some alignment is good enough to get by.

Whatever tempts you, don't give in. Stand strong on our second requirement, alignment of goals. This means accepting nothing less than total 100% alignment of goals.

Total 100% alignment means that you and your business partner can't, for example, be at 80% or 85% alignment on goals. A partnership on those terms won't work.

Actually, in all fairness, it might work initially. You and your partner might be all right for a year or even a few years. But further down the line, problems would definitely surface. Looking, say, a decade out, the differences in your goals versus those of your partner will become too strong to ignore.

As an analogy, it would be like going on a road trip from New York to California. You and your partner may start off in agreement about which road to take. But later on in the trip, you and your partner will find yourselves conflicted. You still want to go to California. But your partner? Turns out he actually wants to go to Chicago.

As you drive along the highway and begin seeing exits leading into downtown Chicago, your partner begins telling you to take one. You don't want to take any of the exits, though. It doesn't make sense to, when your goal is driving to California.

So you keep the car speeding along the interstate, past all of those exits for Chicago. This does not sit well with your partner. Out of desperation, your partner now punches you and tries to grab the steering wheel.

"Are you crazy?"

It sure seems that way. Only a crazy person would fight for the steering wheel while going 70 mph on a busy highway.

You can imagine how this ends. You and your partner could wind up in a fiery car wreck, the kind that makes the six o'clock news and draws rubberneck drivers by the hundreds. Even if a wreck isn't the final outcome, you and your partner will still undoubtedly separate on very, very bad terms.

The fiery car wreck from this analogy is comparable to the way a business can figuratively crash and burn when its partners aren't aligned on goals.

The fight for control of the steering wheel is also closely paralleled in business. You can see it when business partners fight for control over the direction of their business. One partner, for instance, may want the company to hit $100M in revenue. The other partner, like the Chicago-loving passenger, only wants to reach $5M in revenue. These differing goals will inevitably cause the partners to disagree. Their disagreements will only intensify the longer the partnership continues. Eventually, disagreements may reach the level of outright confrontations, hostility, and power grabs. And if our car analogy is any indication, you know how badly the situation will end.

Can you see now why 100% alignment on goals is so essential? You must know from the beginning whether your partner has the same long-term goals for the business as you. I'm talking goals that stretch out over the next 10-15 years. If there's no alignment on goals at this extended scale, then don't partner. If you do, it's like you're jumping in the car with someone who may eventually try to grab the wheel from you on the highway. Be a smart driver and an even smarter business owner by avoiding that scenario.

It's really not that complicated. All you need to do is:

1. Get clear on your potential partner's long-term business goals.

2. Make sure there's alignment between those goals and yours and then,

3. If the alignment isn't 100%, don't partner.

Requirement #3 : Common Hunger

The third requirement for successful partnership is common hunger. This means you and you partner need to have a similar work ethic and drive. You must both be equally hungry.

If you, for example, want to work long hours and sleep on a cot in the office, then your partner needs to be there with you. Not on the cot, of course. But with you in terms of having that same ferocious hunger.

Similarly, if you're not ferociously hungry to work on the business, then your partner can't be either. He or she must have the same lower level of hunger.

At first glance, this might seem obvious. It probably seems like common sense that an insomniac workaholic and a relaxed, nine to fiver aren't going to make good partners. At the very least, they'll probably be at odds over food. The insomniac workaholic's tastes will probably be for ramen noodles, Pop-Tarts, and anything with a hint of caffeine. The relaxed nine to fiver, by contrast might enjoy baklava, Kobe beef sliders, and all the other trendy food they've enjoyed during time away from the office.

Kidding aside, the differences in work ethic and hunger are bound to have even more serious consequences for this partnership. Imagine for a moment the less hungry partner getting a phone call while out at a trendy bistro with friends. It's a Friday night around 10:00 p.m. and the caller is their hungry partner.

She's calling to deliver exciting news. She's been crunching the numbers and has identified some ways to generate additional sales from the company's existing customers. A few more sales here. A few more sales there. And together, it could mean boosting business revenues by a few percentage points.

"Isn't that great?"

"Uh, yeah," says the partner out for dinner. Maybe he means it too. Maybe this relaxed partner really is happy for the discovery his workaholic partner has just made.

But how long can the differences, evident on this Friday night and others, continue? How many more Friday nights will the workaholic partner slave away, alone in the office, while her partner is out being social?

It's only a matter of time, especially since, in this particular example, the workaholic is giving her partner a call. I'm no Sigmund Freud, but I'd bet that there's a psychological reason for the call. It could be that the workaholic partner unconsciously feels alone and needs someone to talk to. She may crave validation too. This goes back to the loneliness I spoke of, and it could easily explain the Friday night phone call.

If nothing else, the workaholic partner is bound to resent being in a partnership with someone who doesn't work as hard as she does. This resentment will eventually kill the partnership.

Like I said, though, this probably seems obvious. Yet you'd be amazed at how many business owners never consider this third requirement, common hunger. Somehow, it never crosses their mind that a partner should be as hungry as they are.

This is why I consider common hunger to be the silent killer of partnerships. If business owners knew to look for it, they'd have no trouble snuffing out this silent killer, killing it before it killed their partnership. Most don't, however, and that's why a lack of shared hunger kills so many promising partnerships.

The partnerships may start out well, just like the partnership in our recent example. Yet check back in a few months, a year, or longer. You'll find then that the differences in work ethic, drive, and hunger will have split the partnership open. The partners will be standing apart, separated, like the ground after an earthquake.

I'm speaking from experience. During my early days as a business owner, I didn't understand the importance of common hunger. My ignorance led me to start a business with a partner who didn't share my voracious appetite. He was sorta hungry, but not hungry enough to eat a horse, as I was.

At the very beginning of our business, this wasn't an issue. My partner and I got off to a smooth start, dividing up the work in a way that seemed fair. My partner was responsible for finding and renovating houses. My responsibilities were then to find and cultivate relationships with buyers for these houses. The buyers I brought in were U.S.-based and international investors who bought our houses as turnkey investments.

Everything seemed clear and on track until about six months into the partnership. That was the point when I looked up from my work. I saw then how much our roles in the partnership had changed.

My role had somehow expanded to include renovating properties. I'd had to take on renovation duties because my partner had abruptly stopped renovating the houses we'd acquired. Talk about a mess. These houses were partially renovated and we couldn't sell them until the renovations were finished. To complete the renovations, I had to jump in, calling contractors and finding new ones.

Sadly, the reality of the renovations issue didn't hit me until the six-month mark. Prior to that point, I'd assumed my partner's inability to supervise the renovations was just a glitch. I saw it as something temporary, like a hiccup in our business. No worries, right?

Wrong. Dead wrong. For I wasn't just lending a temporary hand to my partner. I was doing his part of the business for him.

My partner was happy to let me do it, too. Not that I blame him. I mean, who wouldn't enjoy this kind of lopsided arrangement?

It's a great deal for the partner who isn't as hungry. Yet I was hungry and I needed a partner who was too. I also didn't need dead weight in my business. And my partner in this earlier business was just that: dead weight.

Resolving this situation was, fortunately, not difficult. My partner and I had only been in business for about nine months. In that time, our business hadn't grown very much. We'd done deals, but there weren't any assets to divide. So I was able to easily resolve things with a simple phone call.

I called up my business partner and dissolved the partnership in a short, civil phone call. I said, "Hey, we had an agreement. You were going to handle the renovation and I was going to handle attracting investors, talking to the folks that would be our customers. I'm now doing both and it's not working for me. He agreed that he wasn't doing a good job. I suggested we dissolved the partnership and he agreed. I wasn't attacking him or being rude, so he was OK with calling it a failed partnership and moving on. Our partnership was then officially over.

Hanging up the phone, I remember breathing a sigh of relief. I realized too, just how lucky I'd gotten. It could have been far harder and far more emotional to dissolve the partnership. Somehow, owing perhaps to good luck, I'd done it with just a brief phone call.

It goes without saying that not every partnership ends as easily as that one did. You can't assume yours will either. If you have to end a partnership, you can expect a difficult time. Do yourself a favor and don't get to that point. Take the time at the beginning to properly vet any potential partner.

The four requirements will help you to do that, especially with common hunger. Zooming out a bit, to look again at the four requirements overall, let me reiterate that all four must be met to consider a person viable as a partner. I know I harped on that before, but you need to really understand this. It's so critical. Ignoring it leads you toward failing partnerships like the one I've just described.

That particular partner met three of my four requirements for a partner. He had the same risk tolerance as me, the same goals, and complementary skill sets. All that was missing in my partner was a work ethic similar to mine.

It's not just him, either. Think again about the partnership I described involving my wife in our house flipping business. Remember how the two of us were perfectly aligned on all requirements except identical risk tolerance? There were definite reasons why these two partnerships both ended. And that reason is that my partner and I, in each case, weren't aligned on all four requirements. We may have been partially there, with three out of four, but each partnership was still doomed.

Now then, what about that fourth requirement?

Requirement #4: Complementary Skill Sets

In marriage, the ultimate partnership, we often say that our spouse completes us. You might also hear one spouse refer to the other as her better half. This is one way to express that the right relationship helps those in it to feel complete.

You're not marrying your business partner. But he does need to complete you, albeit in the business sense. And the way your business partner does that is through his skill set. If your partner has a complementary skill set to yours, then congratulations. You've found the kind of business partner who really does complete you.

Conversely, if your business partner has the same skills as you, then you can't expect her to complete you. It's just not possible because the two of you have too much overlap. You may look different, think in different ways, and disagree over Coke vs. Pepsi. But when it comes to business and skill sets, the two of you are practically identical. Whatever small differences exist in terms of skill sets will be too minor to matter. Your company will have two identical leaders.

Why can't you have identical leaders?

Think about one of the benefits of partnering, which we talked about awhile back. We saw that with the right partner, one plus one can equal more than two. It can equal three, four, five, and so on. You remember that, right?

It's this idea that's at play in our fourth requirement for a business partner. You need to make sure your partner completes you with the right skill set. And the right skill set is one that makes the one plus one equation of a partnership amount to something greater than two.

You can't have this equation work out to three or more when your partner is your clone.

To put things another way, it's like your business is a complete person. Each business owner, you included, is part of that person. Maybe a single owner is, metaphorically speaking, half of the person that is the business. The owner must find a partner who can complete the other half of that person, since together these parts will equal one full person, allowing that person, the business, to live and function at full capacity.

Wow, that analogy got spacey and existential really fast. If I lost you, let's bring things back with a more grounded example. Let me remind you about how my business partner complemented me in the area of sales. You've heard all about it before, so no need to rehash things here. I just want to remind you of how my skill set was completed by a partner to form a complete person, our business.

Sales. That was my weak area. What about you? What's your area of weakness? What skill set could a partner bring that would make you and your business complete?

Think about that and let it guide you, along with the other requirements in sizing up your potential business partner.

*

And then?

What happens when you find a potential partner who does meet all four requirements?

Then...you assess them again.

More?

Yes, more. Another step in the process.

Your next step is to take your potential partner out, figuratively-speaking, on a date. The date will be a test project. In this way, you'll be able to see what it's like to work with the person without committing to a long-term partnership.

I call the test project a date because of the parallels to marriage. Excluding what happens in Vegas, marriage is nearly always preceded by dating. You meet your significant other for dinner and a movie, dancing, or some other activity. The idea is to get a feel for how this other person behaves.

You should also, hopefully, have an enjoyable time. But even if you're miserable, the date probably only lasts for an hour or two. That time may seem like an eternity. But it's peanuts in comparison to the time you'd spend in a marriage. It's far less costly, too, since the only expenses would be the costs of the date, like a restaurant meal and movie tickets.

Apply this same idea to business partnerships and you get the concept of the test project. It's how you "date" your partner-to-be. A good test project will have a clear start and end date. That way you can make a smooth and quick exit if the project doesn't work out. But your test project should also be long enough that you can get a feel for your potential partner and how they operate.

How long is long enough? It's longer than one day. Depending on your business, the test project might also need to be longer than a single week or month. In these latter cases, don't worry about the lengthy time frame. It's fine to drag your feet early on in testing out the partnership.

You can, of course, take this to an extreme, with a test project, for example, that lasts several years. Still, assuming you don't go that far, there's nothing wrong with taking your time on the test project.

You can also do more than one test project. It's like how in dating, one successful date can lead to another. Your test project—that date with your potential business partner—can be followed by a second project and a third and so on. Eventually, you'll have done enough of these projects that you'll be able to accurately tell the success potential of working with this person. In addition, you'll know her better personally.

Another reason for test projects is that, in some cases, you might not actually end up completing the project. Your prospective partner might decline to do the test. If that happens, your project can be considered a smashing success. For it's raised a red flag about your partner-to-be, a red flag you might have otherwise missed.

The red flag is your potential partner's reluctance to do the test project. Why doesn't he want to do it? What is he worried you're going to discover about him during the test?

With questions like those, you'd probably be wise to walk away from this potential partnership. It's evident that your partner isn't on the same page as you regarding the partnership. Plus, there's that ominous question of what he's worried about you discovering during the test project.

The right partner, though, will be cool with doing a test project. She'll recognize its importance and she'll see the benefit in assessing you during the project.

Assuming the test project goes well, leading perhaps into other successful projects, then you'll finally have the green light to proceed with the partnership. As you progress toward that point, let me give you seven additional insights related to partnering. These insights will help you connect the dots between all we've discussed so far. This way we can ensure that nothing falls through the cracks as you evaluate partnering and perhaps even move forward with it.

Here's the full list:

1. Partnering is a last resort

2. Use personality assessment tests

4. Have clearly defined roles

5. Review roles and other aspects of the partnership at quarterly meetings

6. Create a buy/sell agreement

7. Join a mastermind

8. Do the obvious thing

Insight #1: Partnering is a Last Resort

Before you partner, consider who you can hire. Chances are there's someone out there you can hire to handle whatever area you're weak in. This is why partnering should be seen as a last resort. It's what you do when you've exhausted all other options.

Adopt this attitude and it'll keep you from winding up with too many business partners. You won't have so many partners that some can just hang out, do nothing, and take a share of the profits from you.

As an analogy, your business won't be like those ridiculously big bands. I'm talking about the music bands where there's like eight people. You know what their music sounds like. But come on, does it really take eight people to make that sound? What's half the band doing? Besides, many musicians barely earn enough as it is, so with eight people in a mildly successful band, how does anyone make any money?

I know, I know. It's all about the vibe and the group dynamic, everybody in the band jamming together in rhythm. It's not just a profitable rhythm. And it doesn't sound like a good way to run any for-profit group, whether a band or a business.

Another problem with having too many band mates or business partners is that it also dilutes your ownership in the business. After all, the business is yours. It's your baby, your pride and joy. Why, then, would you dilute your stake in it? Why split your share of the business so other partners can own a piece of it?

In place of bringing on three partners, you could just hire three employees to help you out. I suppose this goes back to my earlier point in the chapter about the confusion between employees and partners. In case you missed it there, your employees are not your partners. They just aren't. So before you ever think of bringing on a partner — much less three partners — see if you can get by with just hiring more employees.

Notice how I keep saying three partners when describing excessive partnerships? The reason is that to me, three partners or more seems like a sign that the business is in trouble. The obvious exception would be a family business, the sort of business where your partners are your dad and any siblings. That is, however, the one and only one exception.

Insight #2: Use Personality Assessment Tests

Along with the test project and the four requirements, you can also get a feel for your partner by using personality assessment tests. These tests are actual written tests with questions to complete.

Look around online and you can find dozens of them. One that I'd highly recommend is called the Culture Index.

This particular test has made a profound difference for my business partner and me. We've both taken it and the test has shown our respective strengths, weaknesses, and motivations. This knowledge enables us to be more receptive to one another's needs and do a better job of collaborating overall.

Insight #3: Have Clearly Defined Roles

Besides taking the Culture Index, I believe my current partnership has succeeded because my partner and I have clearly defined roles. By understanding our different roles in the business, we're able to avoid having overlap. I know exactly what I'm responsible for, as does my partner. We don't overlap and that's a good thing. For when there is overlap, then everyone becomes responsible for a given task or area. And if everyone is responsible for something, then realistically no one is responsible.

Clearly define everyone's roles, however, in a business partnership, and it's no secret who's in charge of what. You're in charge of outreach and marketing, for example. Your partner is in charge of fulfillment and client orders. This eliminates friction in your business and helps the business accelerate.

Insight #4: Review Roles and Other Aspects of the Partnership at Quarterly Meetings

Your role and your partner's role should be clearly defined (see #3 above). Yet these roles shouldn't be set in stone. Nor should the partnership itself. Instead, you should continually review roles and other aspects of the partnership at quarterly meetings.

These quarterly meetings will contribute to your partnership's continued health. I know this fist-hand from doing quarterly meetings at my own company.

When we do these meetings, my partner and I will meet with others in our company for an entire day. Over the course of that day, we'll discuss our company's goals and outline the agenda for our next quarter. We'll also get clear about our responsibilities, objectives, goals, and anything else that will contribute to the company's success over the next 90 days.

Meeting for an entire day may not sound like fun. But isn't it easier to have a set time when everyone can come together and discuss the business's long-term direction? It sure beats trying to figure that out in a piecemeal way over long emails back and forth, or worse, in your head, with no feedback from your partner and other relevant people in your company.

Insight #5: Create a Buy/Sell Agreement

Silly as it might sound, I have to preface this fifth insight with a legal disclaimer. I'm not a lawyer or a CPA. So while I'm encouraging you here in #5 to create a document that is legally binding (i.e. the buy/sell agreement), I'm not the guy to consult when you create it.

That little disclaimer doesn't mean, though, that I can't explain the buy/sell agreement to you. I'm glad to. Because this document, the agreement, is really important. It's what allows you to easily — or at least, more easily — dissolve a partnership later on.

Like its name suggests, the buy/sell agreement describes the buying/selling of the company. It defines how you and your partner will value the company and handle a cash-out, if that day ever comes.

Without this agreement in place, you're going to have a tough time dissolving the business later on. You may, for example, be 10 years into it, flush with cash, and flushed with anger at the difficulty of ending the partnership.

The cure for this is the buy/sell agreement. Create it when there's no revenue so you and your partner can be prepared when your business eventually reaches, say, $100M in revenue. If that day comes and your partnership ends, then the buy/sell agreement will provide a simple, mechanical way for you and your partner to split up.

While we're on buy/sell agreements, let me also point out that you'll probably need other legally binding documents when partnering. If the business is new, for example, you need to create an operating agreement and other documents in order to start a legal business entity (i.e. LLC, LLP, etc.). Your lawyer will be far more knowledgeable about all this than I am. So let her advise you on the specifics.

Insight #6: Join a Mastermind

This is it, the solution I promised you at the start of this chapter for how to overcome entrepreneurial loneliness. It keeps you from becoming desperate at restaurants and coffee shops as described earlier. And it keeps you from partnering just so you'll have a friend. Masterminds offer folks to hang out with and oftentimes folks to drink with when business isn't going well. Masterminds, then, are the solution to loneliness.

The best mastermind is one where the members are at similar stages of their business. You'll be surrounded, for example, by other people who are also ten months into running their companies.

In a group like this, you'll finally be able to talk with people who can relate to you. The group's members will likely be experiencing all the same agony and ecstasy that you are. They'll know what it's like to be soaring emotionally one day, crashing on another, and lethargic on a third.

Those in your mastermind will also be able to see solutions that you yourself may not see. This point is best explained in a chapter from an obscure little book called *Think and Grow Rich*. Seriously, though, this book has sold bazillions of copies. It sold that many copies because it's really great. It was written by Napoleon Hill and you should read it if you haven't already.

Here's Hill's definition of the Mastermind: "The Mastermind consists of two or more people who work in perfect harmony for the attainment of a definite purpose. It is the principal through which you may borrow and use the education, the experience, the influence and perhaps the capital of other people in carrying out your own plans in life. It is the principle through which you can accomplish in one year more than you could accomplish without it in a lifetime if you depended entirely upon your own efforts for success." (Hill https://www.youtube.com/watch?v=8EQWhQt9OQo)

Valuable as masterminds are, you might not be able to find one. If that's the case, you're not out of luck. You can still go to Meetup.com and find a relevant group to join. The right Meetup group will have people who can relate, on some level, to you and your business struggles.

Incidentally, I am a partner in a real estate investing mastermind. If you'd like more info about that, feel free to reach out to me at mike@JustStartRealEstate.com with the subject line: Mastermind.

Industry events are another option here if the perfect mastermind group doesn't exist. Attend trade shows, conferences, or other events in your industry and you'll rub shoulders with the kind of people who know what you're going through.

If Meetups and industry events don't work, you can try yet another strategy for beating loneliness. This one is to find and talk one-on-one with select business owners. Take them, for example, to lunch or coffee. For the price of a sandwich or a coffee, a meeting like this could give you an experienced, sympathetic listener to bounce ideas off.

Talk to enough business owners like this and you may develop some strong relationships. If these relationships are strong enough, you'll have no trouble doing another more involved strategy for fighting entrepreneurial loneliness.

This strategy is to form your own private board of directors. To create your board, you'll find people you respect—perhaps people from those coffee and lunch meetings. Then you'll form a board of directors and bounce ideas off them.

Your board of directors will function similarly to how a company has its own board of directors. The difference is that in your case, board members aren't giving their opinions on how the company should be run. Rather, they're giving those opinions on how you should personally operate, in business and maybe in life too.

Given the important role they play, your private board of directors can't be made up of flaky, uncommitted members. They must be committed to helping you and willing to sit down with you regularly—once per quarter for an hour, for example.

You can get a sense for people's commitment just by asking them, point-blank, about being on your board of directors. Those who give you maybes and other indecisive answers don't make the cut. You may get a few of these responses, but I'd bet you also get a number of yeses. In fact, you'll probably be amazed by just how many of these people you ask agree to be on your board.

It makes sense because most successful business owners can relate to the struggles of other owners. They've been where you are and find it rewarding to lend you a hand.

You can't expect them to run your business for you. But words of advice and encouragement? Those are well within reach when you have the right board of directors.

Insight #7: Trust Your Gut

I want to give you one more piece of advice about partnering. This advice could probably be printed at the end of each chapter in this book.

You might know what I'm going to say. It's what I emphasized during the chapter on hiring. And I've reiterated it elsewhere since then. You know, the idea of trusting your gut.

That advice is as true in discussions of partnering as it is in every other aspect of business. Your gut matters and you should not ignore it. If your gut is telling you not to partner, don't partner. It doesn't matter that you're desperate for help in your business or think you've found the perfect business partner. What matters is that your gut is sounding the alarm, telling you that partnering is a bad idea.

Are you going to listen? Or are you going to turn a deaf ear?

Similarly, when you're already in a partnership, will you listen to your gut then too? Listening is just as important now as it was when you first considered a partnership. This time around, your gut tells you it may be time to end a partnership.

When you reach that point, you're probably too late. The partnership is probably beyond saving and should have been ended long ago. You've only come to this realization now because your gut finally worked up the courage to tell you.

Your gut, if it can be compared to a person, often lacks the courage to speak openly to you. It knows that you frequently ignore it. Sometimes, though, situations get so bad that your gut can't sit by silently. It has to speak up, as in the situation here with your partnership.

Trust your gut. But don't be hasty either in ending partnerships. There may be times when you're the real source of the problem. I'm not saying you're a bad person. It might just be that the responsibility for the issues in the partnership is more yours than your partner's. If you're responsible, for example, for the company's lead generation and leads aren't coming in, don't blame that on your partner. It's on you.

There are also times when your partner is indeed responsible for failures in the business, yet she has a clear plan for fixing the situation. I had this happen a while ago in my business with sales. Since my partner handles sales, I could have blamed him and jumped to the conclusion that our partnership should be ended. But that would have been rash and uncalled for.

Thinking calmly, I chose instead to discuss the situation with my partner. He owned up to the sales slump and showed me an excellent plan for how he was going to fix the problem. Sure enough, my partner carried out his plan and got our sales back to normal.

This example with my partner reinforces my point about using discretion when trusting your gut. Assess the situation—in this case a partnership—in as much detail as you can. Then if it still seems, in your gut, like the time to end a partnership or avoid one altogether, trust that feeling.

Speaking of trusting your gut, my gut is telling me that it's time to end this chapter. We've covered partnering in enough detail that I believe you'll be ready if/when the time comes.

Let's put aside partnering and turn our attention to another topic. It's the next of those six core concepts we're covering, chapter by chapter, in this book.

Number five, coming right up, is maintenance. Join me in a moment and I'll explain exactly what maintenance means and why it's vital to your business.

Chapter 5 – Maintenance

No hook this time. No lengthy analogies or drawn-out observations either. We're on a roll in our discussion, and an intro along those lines would only kill the mood.

The discussion now continues with a look at our fifth core concept: maintenance.

What's maintenance?

Only the difference between life and death.

You're alive, for example, reading this book because of maintenance. In that case, you've visited a doctor at certain points in the past to get check-ups. The doctor calls those visits checkups, but he might just as easily call them maintenance. The two words are interchangeable. Both describe the process to ensure you're in good working order and not at risk for any life-threatening health problems.

Maintenance isn't just limited to your physical health, though. In fact, when you think about maintenance, you probably associate the word with physical things. Doing a tune-up on a car is a good example to make sure it's safe to drive. Or doing maintenance on the roof of your house to make sure it won't collapse while you're at home asleep.

What about business? This is a business book, after all, so does our life and death idea work in that area?

Yes, it absolutely does. As a business owner, maintenance will mean the difference between life and death for your company. Perform regular maintenance and your company stays in good health. Barring unforeseen events, your company's life won't be in any danger.

Avoid maintenance, on the other hand, and you put your company at risk. Your company becomes like the man over fifty who refuses to get a prostrate exam. Or like the woman who never finds time to do a breast exam.

How, though, do you perform maintenance on your company? This isn't like a doctor's check-up, for example, where you've done it a few times and know what to expect. Nor is it like a car tune-up, where you can just outsource the maintenance to some gear-head at your local garage. Maintenance is something you'll need to understand and then do yourself on a routine basis.

Understanding maintenance begins with defining it. I've given you an overall definition so far, with all this talk of life and death. Now let's get more specific, zooming in to focus on maintenance as it relates to your business.

In business, maintenance means doing the work necessary to ensure that a company and the team running it are both in excellent health.

Notice how we're talking about two different things here. There's the company and then there are the people running the company. The two are viewed separately when you're doing maintenance for your business.

As you perform maintenance on the company, you'll be assessing its health based on various metrics. Your focus may be, for example, on certain metrics related to marketing. That's what my partner and I concentrate on, to a great extent, when doing maintenance on our company. We track marketing metrics to see whether the money we're spending is coming back in the form of real estate transactions. We're also looking at metrics outside of marketing, like cash flow and profit.

While my company happens to be in the real estate industry, don't let that be your excuse to skip tracking company financials. Tracking financials is an industry-agnostic activity. It's something you can and should do regardless of what industry your company happens to be in.

That might sound obvious to you, tracking company financials. It's not exactly earth-shattering news.

You'd be amazed, though, at how many people I see who don't do it. As a business coach, I consistently encounter entrepreneurs who don't believe in actively monitoring their company's financial stats. They seem to think that you can just wing it without watching the numbers.

Winging it is a bad idea because it leaves you completely clueless as to what's going on in your business. You're still aware of the big developments: losing a major supplier, say, or closing a big deal. Yet you're unable to see all the smaller nuances in the business. You may not realize, for instance, that your profits this quarter are only ¾ of what they were a year ago to date.

In this instance, the profits could indicate that your company is sliding backward. Tracking financials would allow you to see this and begin working to solve the problem. Without tracking, though, you're likely to miss this problem and others. You're simply winging it in a state of absolute ignorance.

I like to compare this kind of ignorance to flying a plane. When entrepreneurs don't track their financials, it's like they're flying the plane without an instrument panel.

Is it any wonder that so many entrepreneurs are constantly scared and stressed out about their businesses? Fear and stress are a natural part of being in business. Yet these emotions are going to be much more intense if you're flying the plane of your business without instruments. You can't help but be terrified when there's no telling whether you're flying into a mountain or losing altitude and heading down toward a crash-landing in the ocean.

The way to avoid flying blind is to monitor your company's financials. Follow them on a regular basis, and you'll have a clear sense of your company's health. You'll know what's working and where you need to perform maintenance work.

Speaking of maintenance, there's more to it than just checking up on your company itself. Look back a few paragraphs, and you'll see that maintenance also involves the people running your company.

For this second side of maintenance, you'll be concentrating on the health of the people working for you. I don't mean that you're looking at their physical health. Instead, the idea is that you're focused on your employees' output and state of mind on the job. Those two parts — output and state of mind — are what we'll define as health for employees.

Output means asking whether your employees are performing their work at healthy levels.

What's healthy versus unhealthy in terms of output? You can determine that through tracking activities and results. For example, look at how much time your employees are spending on their activities. Take note of what the results are from the time they've spent. Then, go a step further and incentivize your employees for the results you want.

Incentivizing means rewarding your employees for results. This is important because it sends a message to your employees that results are what count. Going through the motions — a.k.a. doing job-related tasks — isn't enough. The tasks still need to be done, yet rewards only come when the results of the tasks are good or even great.

This point about rewarding results is probably obvious like tracking financials. Still, if you'd watched me early on in my business career, you'd have seen me mistakenly incentivizing activity. I had the false belief that since activity leads to results, incentivizing my employees for doing their activities would translate into great results.

It was only later that I realized the problem with this attitude. I saw that my approach was comparable to a parent who rewards his child for doing homework. The child can rush through the homework, giving incorrect answers or even writing gibberish. Yet she still gets rewarded for completing the homework. That's what it was like for me, rewarding my employees for completing activities versus getting results.

Aware of the problem at last, I changed my approach to the one we've just discussed: incentivizing based on results and not activities.

*

Zooming out a little bit, let's get back to our earlier point. We'd been talking about the health of your employees. Output is one aspect of that, and we've just covered it. Now here's the other part: state of mind while on the job.

This part of maintenance involves assessing where your employees are, mentally, and whether that's a good place. In a sense, it's like you're becoming the company shrink. No one's going to lie on a couch in your office. But you're still going to be asking questions and doing a ton of listening, all in the interest of finding out what's on your employees' minds.

Being the company shrink, albeit unofficially, is harder today than it was decades ago. In the 1980's, for example, you could get by with just an open door policy. You'd tell your employees, "My door is always open," and they'd often come talk to you. It was an easy way to find out what was on your employees' minds without you having to do much work.

Today, on the other hand, you can't rely on the open door policy. Times have changed so much that it just doesn't work anymore. People nowadays won't come to you simply because they know your door is always open, whether in the literal or figurative sense. Instead, you have to go to them.

Does that make you uncomfortable, the thought of going up to your employees unannounced and trying to determine what's on their minds? It sounds like a very awkward exchange, especially if you are introverted or don't consider yourself a people person.

Your own sense of discomfort is nothing, however, compared to what your employees would feel if they had to come to you. Think about it from their perspective. Your door may be open, but your employees would still have to make the uncomfortable choice to walk into your office. Often, they'd need to work up the courage to do so. And there's the added risk of coworkers seeing them enter your office and wondering what's wrong.

Considering the negatives, your employees aren't likely to approach you and share how they're feeling about being at work. This is why I say you need to go to them. Take the initiative and do it.

In terms of exactly what to do, I recommend having one-on-one meetings every week with each member of your team. That's what I do with my staff.

We covered one-on-one meetings a few chapters ago, but I believe it's worth mentioning them again. The reason is that the meetings are a simple yet powerful way of going to your employees and monitoring their psyches.

When I have these one-on-one meetings, they're always held outside of the office. I purposely avoid having the meetings in conference rooms or other spots around our office. Those sorts of places are too close to the hustle and bustle of work. There's no sense of true detachment by employees when we meet in the office. Employees will still feel as though they're at work, despite the fact that the one-on-one meeting is not about work-related topics. The only solution is to leave the office. Go somewhere close yet far away in the sense that it doesn't feel like you're at work.

An example of such a place would be the large atrium in the building where my company is located. Our atrium is a perfect spot for one-on-one meetings, with its park benches and positions outside of earshot. When I take employees out to the atrium for one-on-one meetings, they get a sense of being away from the office without us having to drive a lengthy distance.

Sitting in the atrium during the one-on-one meeting, each employee will have thirty minutes to talk about absolutely anything. Absolutely anything means absolutely anything. There's no limit imposed on what an employee can bring up for conversation.

If they want to spend the time talking about sports, or at the opposite extreme, gardening (is gardening the opposite of sports?), then either of those subjects is what we'll be discussing. I'm personally not into gardening, but I can get interested if doing so will allow me to connect with my employees and get a sense of where they're at mentally.

My desire to connect with employees and understand their mental state also explains why I'll willingly listen to non-work related rants during the thirty-minute meetings. Normally, I don't have time or patience to hear such rants. I don't want to hear, for example, about all the stupid things that a person's spouse did over the weekend, how he parked his car at Costco and didn't remember to get the number of the parking space so it took over an hour to find the car.

Rants like that — about the spouse and his car — normally bore me. But in a one-on-one meeting, I'm happy to sit and listen to them. This is because such rants provide context around why my employees interact as they do with others on the job.

An employee who rants about fights with her spouse is clearly angry. The incident angered her so much that she hasn't been able to let it go and has taken the problem to work. Knowing this, I'm not as surprised later on when I learn that this employee got into a heated argument with one of her coworkers.

The argument may seem like it comes out of the blue. Nonetheless, I know that it's actually the result of this employee's frustration with her dumb spouse, bringing her anger to work and taking it out on others.

Sadly, this isn't much different from the way kids behave in school. If a child gets yelled at by his parents at home, he may take his anger from this experience to school. This is even more apparent in cases where children are physically beaten at home and then end up bullying others at school.

Our job then, as company leaders, is to root out the anger/resentment. We must become aware of its existence and understand why it's there in the first place. That happens by monitoring our employees' mental states through approaches like the 30-minute one-on-one meeting.

The process of monitoring, as I'm describing it, can be compared to crediting a bank account. The bank account is the relationship you have with each of your employees. Since you'll probably have multiple employees, you'll have multiple bank accounts. You'll also likely have bank accounts outside of work, representing the relationships you have with your spouse, kids, and adult friends. As this is a business book, we're going to discuss bank accounts strictly in terms of your relationship with your employees. But know that this concept applies to your relationships outside of work too.

Each relationship you have with an employee is a figurative bank account. Like any bank account, you never want the balance in these accounts to go below zero. If the balance in any of your relationship bank accounts does fall below zero, you're going to have a bad relationship.

The way to avoid having this sort of rocky relationship is to constantly be crediting your relationship bank accounts. By crediting the accounts, I mean that you're actively contributing to them.

With a normal bank account, you might contribute say, $500 each month, putting the money in to help grow the account. For a relationship bank account, you'll contribute intangibles to make the relationship grow.

Contributing intangibles sounds vague, though, doesn't it? It does to me, so I won't stop there in my explanation of crediting relationship bank accounts. Here are a few concrete ways that you can do it.

The most immediate way that comes to mind is the scheduled one-on-one meetings. Each meeting is a credit to that employee's account which is the relationship between you two.

Another way you can credit relationship bank accounts is through reinforcing what your company stands for. Reinforcement happens by reminding employees why they do what they do. You make it clear to them that their work on the job matters and that it furthers a specific worthwhile outcome.

Reminders are important because there's a chance your employees have forgotten what the company stands for. Or if they do remember, it's only a vague memory, a memory that flickers like a small candle rather than burning brightly in their minds like a roaring bonfire. Reminding your employees of what the work they're doing is all about will restore that bonfire.

In my own company, I do this by continually reminding my employees that they're in the business of helping people. Helping others is why we do what we do. It's what drives us to find motivated sellers and help them get rid of real estate they don't want, real estate that, quite often, they've inherited and have absolutely no use for.

To people in that position, our services come as a major relief. We're seen almost like rescuers, helping them escape from a bad real estate situation.

Putting it in these terms gives employees a clear sense of why we do what we do at my company. There's no mystery around our company's why, especially not with my continually reminding them.

Follow my lead here and make sure you're doing the same. It's an immediate and easy way to credit the relationship bank accounts you have with your employees. The accounts, in this instance, get credited because your employees feel a deeper connection with you. You may be their superior, but you're still united with them in pursuit of the company's purpose.

A third way to credit relationship bank accounts is through admitting fault, meaning you tell your employees when you're wrong.

At first glance, admitting fault doesn't seem like a means of crediting the accounts. It sounds instead like you're weakening them, destroying whatever good will has been built up through an admission that you're wrong.

The funny part, however, is that weakness actually produces strength. So when you confess your weakness — that you were wrong — it fortifies the relationship.

Why?

Well, just think about jerky bosses you've had in the past. Or, if you've been blessed to escape such bosses, think about jerky teachers, sports coaches, or others you've reported to.

In each instance, one of the main things you probably disliked about this jerk — whoever he was — is that he was supposedly never wrong.

If it were a boss, for example, and he botched one of the company's deals, he wouldn't own up to it. The buck wouldn't stop there. It would stop instead with you or one of your colleagues, even if the boss was clearly at fault.

No wonder you hated him or anyone else in your past in a leadership role who didn't just come out and admit when he was wrong.

But how easy is it for you to do that? Now that the tables have been turned and you're the boss, can you admit when you're wrong? If you can, then you'll be giving your relationship bank accounts — the ones you have with your employees — a major deposit.

The relationships will skyrocket in value because your employees will come to a new understanding of you. They'll realize that while you're the boss, you're not pretending to be some flawless, holier-than-thou leader. No, you're a human being just like them and you're not afraid to admit it.

With this understanding, your employees will generally come to trust you more, let their own guards down, and support your efforts to develop a deeper relationship with them.

Along with admitting fault, there's one more way I'd recommend that you credit your relationship bank accounts. This additional way is to emphasize to your employees how they can win the day.

Winning the day means kicking ass and taking names. It means having the kind of day where you go in and crush it. If you have sales calls to make, for example, you murder those sales calls. If you have research to do, you annihilate that research. And if you have paperwork to complete, you destroy it. But not the actual papers. They're important.

Sounds like a good day, doesn't it? A violent day too. But that's just how we tend to describe being productive today. In bizarrely violent terms.

Even without such terms, you know the kind of day I've just described. It's a day where you win.

Hopefully you've had plenty of these kinds of days yourself. But what about your employees? How are they doing when it comes to winning the day? And do they even know how to go about winning it?

Chances are your employees lack a clear sense of how they can win the day. This creates an excellent opportunity for you as a leader. You can step in and show your employees what they can do today to feel as though they've won. Point out a couple of things they can do to create the win. Then, help them to create a chain of successful days.

As the days add up, your employees will continually feel great at work. They'll enjoy the feeling of winning on a regular basis, especially since you'll be recognizing them for it.

Make sure you do that too: recognize your employees for their successes. It'll help your employees to see that their victories matter. In addition, providing recognition will also earn you their respect and admiration. Your employees will deeply appreciate that you've provided recognition for their wins and showed them how to win in the first place. With their appreciation, you'll receive major credits to the relationship bank accounts.

Credit the accounts in any of the ways we've just seen, and you'll be on much stronger footing when things go wrong. It will be easier for you to talk to your employees about whatever has gone wrong because you have a balanced relationship with them.

In a relationship that's balanced, you talk to your employees in both the good times and the bad. You don't only go to them when problems arise. Instead, your interactions with them and the lines of communications in general are already well established.

As a result, when problems arise, your employees will know you as a person beyond the scope of the problems. They'll know, for example, that you're not a high-and-mighty jerk, the sort who's never wrong. A few of your employees may also remember your kind words from last week's meeting when you recognized their efforts in front of the group.

These examples constitute credits in the relationship bank account that you have with the employees. Depending on the problem, these credits may be enough to smooth things over. If not, you can withdraw more credits, assuming you've indeed been crediting the account.

Crediting accounts relates, again, to the idea of this chapter: maintenance. Getting back to maintenance in general, let's talk next about why it matters. If the discussion so far hasn't tipped you off, here's a specific example about how and why maintenance matters.

Look at marriage. Once you're married, that's supposedly the end. You and your spouse will be together until, as wedding vows proclaim, "Til death do us part." Yet most marriages today in the U.S. end in divorce. So it's evident that getting married is not in fact a permanent final resting place for couples in their romantic relationship. A marriage can, and often does, end.

I can't speak to all the reasons why marriages end. What I can tell you, though, from personal observation, is that a lack of maintenance seems to be the leading cause of death, at least among those marriages I've seen end.

Maintenance in a marriage means remembering your significant other's birthday and the date of your anniversary. It also means doing those little things each day, like greeting your spouse with warmth and affection when you arrive home from work.

Each of these actions and many more helps to maintain your marriage. This is because the actions continually remind your spouse that you still love and appreciate her. Your spouse realizes that your love and appreciation for her didn't end on the day after your wedding. Those feelings of love and appreciation persist despite the passing of time and despite whatever problems may arise.

If you can get your marriage to the point I've just described, it's highly likely to last. You and your spouse won't end up in divorce court as bitter enemies.

It won't be easy, though. Maintenance almost never is. You have to put in work, difficult work at times. But the payoff is worth it, whether we're still talking about a marriage or thinking again in terms of your business.

For your business, maintenance keeps your employees motivated and in good spirits. Your employees are continually reminded, as the spouse was, of your love and appreciation for them. This translates into lower turnover and a healthy culture in your business. It also causes the KPIs for the business itself to be good and potentially great.

About the KPIs. It's funny how they tend to take care of themselves when you take care of your relationships with employees. The KPIs take care of themselves in the same way as the score seems to take care of itself for certain football teams that win the Super Bowl. Those football teams aren't necessarily the ones with the most talent on paper. What makes the difference, though, is that the teams have great leaders and a rock-solid culture. The result is the members of the team rising to the occasion, winning the Super Bowl despite the odds.

With the football example as well as the earlier one involving marriage, you can probably see now — really, truly see — why maintenance matters. It matters and you've got to do it. End of story.

*

Actually, it's not really the end.

We can't stop the discussion about maintenance just yet. Otherwise you'd be at risk of doing it the wrong way.

Maintenance can be done wrong, for example, if you approach it with the belief that your employees care as much about the business as you do.

Remember that flawed belief? We covered it earlier in this book. I bring it up now because this belief could lead you to do less maintenance than what's actually needed. You might try to skate by with less maintenance because your employees already obviously share your passion for the business.

The reality, though, is that they don't. Few if any employees do.

This can be confusing since people often claim to love the company where they work. Yet what they actually love isn't the company itself. They're in love with the people at the company and the acknowledgment they receive while on the job. That's what loving a company really means.

Consider those two things — people and acknowledgment — and you'll see that both are tied to maintenance. Therefore, if you want people to love your company, you'll need to concentrate on maintenance.

*

A second way you could mishandle maintenance is by assuming that everyone in your business is money-motivated. This idea should also sound familiar to you from earlier in the book.

Here, with maintenance, assuming that your employees are all money-motivated can lead you to try and do maintenance using money. You might, for example, try to maintain your relationship with employees by throwing a $10,000 raise at them. I've been guilty of this, and I've also seen other entrepreneurs do it.

We've all collectively failed, though, because employees in nearly any business will not be purely money-motivated. They'll likely be motivated to a greater extent by the intangibles of working at the business. Intangibles would include the relationships they have with other employees, the company's charitable focus, and the autonomy they receive on the job.

Since these kinds of intangibles are what ultimately drive your employees, you can't use money to cheat on maintenance. Instead, you've got to roll up your sleeves and get your hands dirty.

You also can't cheat on maintenance by just firing and replacing employees.

If that's your idea of doing maintenance, then you're being lazy. You're using firing and replacing to avoid doing the necessary maintenance of developing a person in your business.

I can't blame you, though, for doing that. As a fellow business owner, I realize how tempting it is to just fire and replace. It seems easier to just chuck a "bad" employee and find a new one. Yet this is usually more expensive in the long run, and it can result in frequent stops and starts in a business.

Are there times to fire and replace employees? Absolutely. The problem employee I had whom I've brought up throughout this book is a prime example.

Nonetheless, for every one of those employees — the bad apples, rotten to the core — there may be even more employees who simply need to be developed. These employees could be turned into performers, perhaps high performers, if we'd only spend some time developing them.

*

From maintenance-related mistakes, let's talk now about something even more important. This would be the matter of actually doing maintenance.

If you're a total newbie to maintenance, having never done anything even remotely like it, don't worry. While maintenance will radically transform your business, you don't have to do anything radical in order to get started on it. You can begin by simply scheduling recurring one-on-one weekly meetings with each of your employees.

Schedule the meetings and then make sure they happen. I mean it too. Don't let the one-on-one meetings get pushed around by day-to-day developments in your business. Apart from your office burning down, there's not much else that should get in the way of holding the one-on-one meetings with your employees each week. Those meetings are sacred. They happen no matter what, like the "date night" that many married couples have. Or the schedule that an Olympic-caliber athlete follows when training.

In the instance of the athlete, if Mondays are, for example, a lift day, she lifts. The athlete may have gotten an hour less of sleep the night before. It may be snowing. Yet the athlete still goes to the gym for lifting on Monday at the designated time. It's just what she does.

Your weekly one-on-one meetings with employees need to be the same way. They're just what you do.

As for what you're actually doing at the meetings, it's just to talk. Talk, as we said earlier, about nearly anything.

To have a conversation like that, it'll be necessary for you to remind your employees that the one-on-one meeting is not a business meeting. Make sure they're aware that the two of you are just meeting for a casual, informal chat.

"A casual informal chat? What's the catch?"

Your employees probably won't say that out loud. But internally, they'll be saying it to themselves. The alarm bells will probably be ringing in their heads.

Such a reaction is to be expected. You can't fault your employees for being suspicious of your supposed casual, informal chat. It seems like a trick done for some sinister hidden motive, sort of like the good cop routine that police do. This would be the routine where a police officer befriends a suspect, giving the person a cup of coffee, say, and often appearing to save the suspect from a bad cop, who is really the good cop's partner. The goal of the good cop/bad cop routine is to break down a suspect and get him to confess.

What about you, the employer? Are you trying to break the employee down? Or might this be the windup for a sucker punch of some sort? Is it the calm before you tell the employee that he's fired or that you're lowering his salary?

In truth, none of the above applies to your one-on-one weekly meeting. The meeting isn't driven by anything other than a genuine desire to maintain healthy relationships with your employees. This won't be apparent to your employees at first, so you may need to do most of the talking during the initial meetings.

As you talk, I recommend opening up about your personal life. When you do, you'll show your employees that it's fine for them to talk about their personal life during the meetings too.

What happens, though, if you still have an employee who resists? The person refuses to open up at the weekly meetings, fearing that you're up to no good in spite of ample evidence to the contrary.

For an employee like that, I recommend reassessing whether you still need her. The employee's resistance may be a sign that she's not a fit for your company. If so, your maintenance efforts through the weekly meetings have just proven successful. You've found a problem in your business, thanks to maintenance.

*

Having a casual chat with your employees one at a time during weekly meetings is what I recommend to you as your first step in doing maintenance. Where you go from there will depend on your personality and the nature of your particular business.

With maintenance being dependent on your personality and your business situation, I can't give you any ironclad guidance on how much maintenance is too much. I wish this were possible because maintenance does seem like an area where you could go overboard.

You probably don't want to be so casual and chat so much with employees about off-topic stuff that it kills your focus on the business. So there needs to be a line you draw between being a friend to your employees and being their boss.

As a boss myself, I draw the line at going out and getting drunk with employees. That's a line I won't cross. To me, that's going too far to the friend side. If I go that far, my employees will be shocked later if I have to discipline them.

"I thought we were friends," they'll think.

That's not a conversation I'm willing to have. I want to be able to do what's needed for my company without being so close to my employees that performing the necessary actions becomes difficult. If I end up in that situation and find it difficult to act, then I've failed.

Nonetheless, let me reiterate that my views on becoming close with employees are my own, and yours may well be different. What I consider as too close to employees may be comfortable for you. Know then, that this area — closeness with employees — will vary, especially if you're running a family-owned business.

*

Moving on, I want to give you a tip for becoming more effective at doing maintenance. I'd call this a pro tip, as blogs often do, yet that term has always seemed stupid to me. It suggests that all other articles or written pieces were done by amateurs and aren't worth paying special attention to. And if that's true, then the author shouldn't waste your time with a full article. They should leave the pro tip or two and end things right there.

So no pro tips here. End of rant.

My tip for you about being more effective with maintenance is to multipurpose your interactions with employees.

Interacting with employees is how you do maintenance to begin with. Yet there's nothing saying you have to only do maintenance by itself. You can take other interactions with your employees and turn those interactions into additional opportunities for maintenance.

As an example, I'll frequently use my Monday morning meetings — those with the entire group — as a chance to do maintenance. The meetings will naturally be focused on our company. But time before the meetings start? That's time for maintenance.

In the ten or so minutes before the beginning of the meeting, I can go into maintenance mode with my employees. I'll chat them up about how their weekends went. Or, being in Michigan, I might bring up our beloved football team, long considered the best in the NFL: the Detroit Lions.

These are just a few things I could mention to make conversation right before the Monday meeting starts. With these conversation topics, I'm squeezing maintenance into an unused space.

You can do the same, both at meetings and elsewhere. The key is to look for opportunities, usually unscheduled ones, when you can slip into what I call maintenance mode. These are the instances when you're able to slide a credit or two into the relationship bank accounts with your employees.

You probably won't have to look hard to find opportunities for slipping into maintenance mode and crediting the accounts. There are an infinite number of those opportunities each day.

If you can hold the door for an employee on the way into a meeting, that's an opportunity.

If you're able to bring someone a document they've printed off the printer without being asked to, there's another opportunity.

If you can smile and give a warm, cheerful greeting to one of your employees in the hallway, that would be — you guessed it — yet another opportunity.

And so on. Opportunity after opportunity after opportunity. With each one, you can potentially take a little moment and repurpose it to serve both business and maintenance.

While we're on repurposing, it's worth pointing out that this approach allows you to be lazy. You can be lazy because with repurposing, you're not creating new interactions. Rather, you're seizing the opportunity inherent in interactions that were already happening.

Take the example of me doing maintenance before a group meeting. In this instance, I was going to interact with my employees before the meeting anyway. So it was simply a matter of seizing the opportunity or letting it slip away.

If I'd let the opportunity slip away, I have refrained from making small talk before the meeting. My interaction with the employees would have been cold, with all of us sitting in silence before the meeting.

An interaction like this would constitute a wasted opportunity along with an instance of me debiting my relationship bank accounts with employees.

My employees might not think much of my pre-meeting silence. It's only that those sorts of interactions add up. The interactions form a chain, or more accurately a noose that can eventually strangle you as a leader.

You can end up gasping in disbelief, for example, at how one of your employees could abruptly jump ship for another job elsewhere. How could they pack up and leave without any notice?

How? Because the employee didn't feel like he had much of a relationship with you. The relationship bank account had few credits. As a result, this employee had no qualms about leaving your company as soon as a better opportunity presented itself.

To prevent a scenario along these lines, make sure you're constantly crediting the relationship bank accounts of all your employees. Do it so much that you're practically an account-crediting fanatic.

Your fanaticism in crediting the accounts may not be noticed immediately by your employees. That's OK, though, because this is a long-term campaign.

Thinking long-term, you're working to instill a feeling in the minds of your employees that you've consistently been good to them.

And if you have, then your employees may just think twice about quitting on a dime for a job elsewhere. You'll also reap other benefits like having a better, more productive workplace and a healthier company overall.

Those benefits are waiting for you if you'll only do maintenance. So do it. Become that so-called account-crediting fanatic. Keep close tabs, as well, on the numbers in your business itself. That was the other part of maintenance in addition to the people-focused part.

Practice maintenance in both of these ways simultaneously. Over time, it'll become a habit. You'll find yourself doing maintenance, both scheduled and unscheduled, without breaking a sweat. It's a great place to reach, as a leader, and I believe you can get there.

The chapter you've just read is the first step. It'll get you started, and you can then refine your efforts as you experiment with maintenance, seeing what works and what doesn't in your particular business.

Get started on maintenance, but don't stop reading this book just yet. We still have another core concept to discuss. The next core concept — our final one, in fact — is waiting for you in the following chapter.

In the chapter to come, we'll be exploring the deceptively simple concept of mentors. At first glance, this concept sounds so obvious that you may wonder why it's even in this book. Or worse, you may think I've run out of material and need filler for a sixth principle. Fortunately, that's not at all true. Five, six, and seven all work as numbers for lists of key concepts. So I could have easily stopped at five concepts if the sixth core concept wasn't needed.

Core concept #6 is needed, however, and you're about to see why. Join me on the following page as we start discussing mentors.

Chapter 6 – Mentors and Masterminds

This could all end in a train wreck.

For me and for you as well.

In my case, the train wreck could be me butchering the ending to this book. I could totally muck up this chapter, our last one together, by filling it with cringe-worthy clichés and feel-good platitudes.

If you've read any business books, you probably know what I'm getting at. Far too many of those books end with authors spouting worn-out lines like, "Enjoy the journey!" or "Have fun!"

As if that wasn't bad enough, such books often jam a warm fuzzy story into their last chapter, the kind of story that's supposed to tug at readers' hearts, leaving them feeling happy and perhaps imparting a seemingly deep life lesson.

You probably don't want an ending like that. Even if you do, I'm not going to give it to you. I refuse to write a weak closing chapter, regurgitating the same stale sentimental crap that you've been beaten over the head with elsewhere.

If I did that, it would be a waste of your time, not to mention a terrible way to close out this book. It would also kill my credibility. You'd realize that I'd sold out and you'd probably discount the ideas in this book. And if that happened, this would all end in a train wreck.

What about you, though? How might this all end in a train wreck for you?

In your case, the train wreck might come later on.

To set the scene, let's assume you got started as an entrepreneur. You went into action, following this book's core message to Just Start.

As a result, you established a business and got a few clients or customers. Money came in too. Not millions of dollars. Not hundreds of thousands. But enough that you could concentrate on your business full-time, rather than doing it as a so-called side hustle.

That all sounds pretty good, doesn't it? Sure, and to be fair, it's more than most people ever accomplish. Yet it could still end in a train wreck.

Your train wreck would come from working hard in isolation. You'd be putting in hard work but doing it without having anyone more experienced around to act as a sounding board.

Without the benefit of a more experienced entrepreneur to hear your ideas and offer guidance, you'd inevitably stumble. There would simply be things you didn't know that you need to know. In the absence of this knowledge, you'd likely spin your wheels as a business owner, getting frustrated, especially if your business seemed trapped at a certain level. Under mounting frustration, you might then either give up the business or else you'd keep calm and carry on, pulling long hours and never quite breaking through.

Giving up or soldiering on in vain both represent train wrecks. To avoid either of them, you'll need to seek out a more experienced entrepreneur, someone who's been there, done that and found success in the field of business that you're pursuing.

In more succinct terms, you'd describe this kind of person as a mentor. This chapter will focus on how you find a mentor, how to enlist the person's help, and more.

By discussing mentors and coaches, we can use this last chapter to further empower you. You'll be empowered to find help long after you've finished reading this book and the inevitable challenges come up in your business. When those challenges do arise, you won't be headed for a train wreck. Instead, you'll be headed to your Rolodex or headed online to find who can mentor you through the difficulty.

There is, however, one major issue. It's a huge one that hangs over this chapter's discussion of mentors. The issue is that I offer a paid mentoring/mastermind program.

It comes as no surprise then that I'd be encouraging you to get a mentor. Of course I'd tell you to find one, right? To speak negatively of mentors wouldn't make sense financially. I'd be steering you away from potentially paying me to mentor you.

Sorry if I'm being too blunt here. But it would be wrong to write this whole chapter about mentoring without being up front with you about what I offer.

Don't worry, I'm not going to launch into a description now of mentoring packages and plans. All that matters is that I disclose here that I do offer mentoring. What that consists of, how much it costs, and how you can "Act now!" are completely irrelevant for our discussion here. If you're curious, you can...

...figure it out for yourself; my email is at the end of the book.

End of discussion.

Now, talking seriously about mentors, let's begin.

We'll start with a description of what that even means. What exactly a mentor is.

The simplest definition I can give you for mentor is the following. A mentor is a person who has a level of success that you aspire to and is able to provide you with meaningful, constructive guidance.

Who exactly that person ends up being will depend on your own situation. If you're in real estate, flipping houses for example, your mentor might be someone who's built a multi-million-dollar house flipping business.

In another case, you might be an SaaS (software as a service) entrepreneur looking to scale your fledgling start-up to seven figures. In this instance, your mentor could be a veteran entrepreneur who's successfully exited (i.e. built and sold) multiple tech start-ups.

Whatever your situation, you need a mentor. Otherwise, you're setting yourself up for the kind of train wreck scenario I mentioned at the start of this chapter.

That isn't just speculation on my part. Nor is all this talk of train wrecks meant as a scare tactic to manipulate you into getting a mentor.

When I say you need a mentor, I'm speaking from first-hand experience. Look at my history, and you'll see that I used to be against paying for mentors/masterminds. I thought that mentors, coaches, and masterminds weren't needed.

Why would you pay someone — in money and/or sweat equity — to coach you along? Surely you can figure things out for yourself, especially when everything you need to know is just a few clicks away on the Internet.

Those were my thoughts about mentors when I started my business back in 2008. At the time, I knew I didn't want a mentor. What I didn't know, though, was how to succeed in my chosen field: flipping houses.

Somehow, I managed to do my first successful deal. This deal, as with any house flip deal, involved buying a house, renovating it, and selling it for a profit. As one deal turned into two deals, two deals into three, and so on, I began to get the hang of it. I developed a basic understanding of what I thought it took to run a successful house flipping business.

My understanding was helped, in some cases, by attending monthly meet-ups for real estate investors in my community. At these events, I met other entrepreneurs who'd succeeded in real estate, whether with house flipping businesses or other real estate-related ventures.

Yet these same events — the monthly real estate meet-ups — could also be highly frustrating experiences. I remember talking to fellow attendees, many of whom were quite successful, and feeling as though they were holding back.

When I'd ask these attendees questions in areas where I was having difficulty, they'd often respond with vague answers.

Now to be fair, it would have been unreasonable on my part to expect everyone I talked with at these casual events to perfectly answer my questions.

At the same time, however, was it really so unreasonable to expect that some of the people I met at a given event would be able to provide insightful answers? Particularly when I looked presentable, wasn't being pushy, and had thought out my questions ahead of time?

No, not really.

The fact is that my fellow attendees could have provided far better answers than they did. Why they didn't is something only they know. I suspect it came from a fear of competition. They may have feared saying something that I would then use to become as successful or even more successful than they were. Better to remain tight-lipped and dish out general answers.

If they wanted to play that game, then fine. It wasn't going to stop me. I'd done successful deals and knew how to do a Google search. So I felt confident finding the answers to my own questions, whether through online research or reflecting on past experiences.

Unfortunately, experience is not always the best teacher. This is because you can often have an experience and then interpret it the wrong way. When that happens, you've missed the lesson that experience was trying to teach you.

As a simple example, let's say you're trying to ice-skate. You put on some skates and step out on the ice rink. Right away you slip and fall. You then get back up, holding onto the railing of the rink. Steadying yourself, you try to skate forward. Again, you fall on the ice. OK, maybe the third time is the charm, as the saying goes. You make a third attempt, but this too ends in a fall.

From these experiences, you could easily come to the conclusion that ice-skating isn't for you. That would be a logical interpretation of what's happened. You went out on the ice, tried skating, and fell repeatedly. So the lesson seems to be that you can't ice-skate.

Still, aren't there other people who can ice-skate? Other people just like you? You know the answer. Of course there are.

What separates you from these people, the ones who can ice-skate, is primarily their interpretation of ice-skating experiences. Unlike you, these successful ice-skaters had the experience of falling and then interpreting it as a temporary thing. Falling, to most of them at least, was simply part of learning to ice-skate. Filled with this knowledge, they kept on trying and eventually they succeeded at ice-skating.

The takeaway here is, again, that experience can fail as a teacher if you, the student, interpret your experiences the wrong way. Getting back to my story, this was the problem with me trying to go it alone and letting my experiences be a primary guide in growing my business.

The other guide I relied on, the Internet, was just as problematic. For while the Internet could provide me with the right answers, there were plenty of wrong answers too. And with billions of these answers — right and wrong — waiting for me online, there was no way to make sense of them all.

If I'd had a mentor in those days, I'd have been better equipped to handle the information I found online. My mentor could have helped me curate and verify my findings. Drawing on that person's own successes, the mentor could have steered me away from bad information and toward real answers.

A mentor would also have been able to save me six years of struggling. That's how long I spent trying to figure out for myself how to scale my business, how to get it to the so-called next level where it would become worth millions of dollars.

Granted, six years is shorter than other famous struggles. My six years are nothing, for example, compared to forty years. That's how long the Israelites from the Bible wandered in the desert.

God (pun intended), I can only imagine being out there, lost in the desert, tired, confused, and angry. Feeling as though nothing you're doing is working.

Actually, that doesn't sound too different from my own six-year struggle, minus the desert part.

The bottom line is that if I'd had a mentor, I would not have struggled, at least not nearly to the extent that I did, for those six years.

With 20-20 hindsight, I can now say unequivocally that a mentor would have made the difference early on. I'm confident about this because of what happened when I finally got a mentor. That was in 2015, nearly seven years into my business.

At that time, I had just launched a podcast called *Just Start Real Estate* (shameless plug), and was introduced to a fellow house flipper named Justin Williams. Justin was flipping several times the number of houses as me. One hundred houses per year, compared to my twenty-five.

The interesting part, though, was that Justin claimed to have lots of free time. He supposedly had time to travel and be with friends and family.

Since Justin lives in California, it was hard for me to verify what he was saying. Maybe he really was working less and still crushing it in his business. But it might also have been exaggeration.

Only with time did the truth emerge. I slowly got to know him, becoming familiar enough with him to see that he wasn't lying or exaggerating. This guy was the real deal.

As the truth came out, Justin offered me a coaching program. There was no material (workbooks, exercises, etc.), little in the way of structure, and no guarantee of success. All this coaching program consisted of were a few meetings each year, a Facebook group, and access to Justin, the house flipper I'd gotten to know, along with another super-successful real estate investor, Andy McFarland.

Oh, and there was also a price tag. Can't forget that part of the coaching program. Not when a year of the program cost $25,000. That's college tuition, when you think about it. It's equivalent to the down payment you might make on a house.

To pay that kind of money for a year of unstructured coaching seemed crazy. But what was the alternative? Trade the year of coaching for another year of struggling to take my business to the next level? Besides, if I could just do two more deals during the year, then the coaching program would pay for itself!

So I paid the money. Or rather my business partner, Mike (confusing huh?) and I paid it together. We came into the coaching program as a pair, and we soon got on the first call with Andy.

That first call...

You're going to think I'm exaggerating, but that first call was really a game-changer. I mean that. It's the truth, not just a convenient part of the story.

The first call began with Mike and I telling Andy about our business. We filled him in on what we were up to and our efforts to take the business to million dollar levels. After that, Andy showed us how his own business operated.

Unlike the people I'd met at real estate meet-ups, my coach wasn't tight-lipped. He openly explained what he had done to take his business from $300,000 to $3,000,000. Andy gave us his entire playbook, so to speak, over the course of the call. It was all right there: what he'd done and what it would take for our business to scale up from $250,000 per year.

Following the call, Mike and I had a choice to make. We could take the insights we'd gained from the call and treat them as food for thought, incorporating some of what we'd learned, while casually considering the rest. Or we could apply it all aggressively to our business.

We chose the latter, taking the coach's playbook from the call and running with it. The result? Our business went to $1,000,000 revenue in just twelve months.

We grew at the kind of astronomical hockey-stick rates that are the fantasy of every entrepreneur. It was unreal. And, in a shameless plug for mentoring, our growth had all come about from that initial call. The two hours we'd spent on the phone during that call with our coach basically set the stage for our growth.

If you want to quantify it, I'd estimate about 50% of the growth can be attributed to lessons learned on that call. Those lessons were then expanded upon in the ensuing year on more calls, Facebook interactions, and in-person meet-ups. Yet it all started on Call #1.

In fact, it was the year of jaw-dropping growth and the call that kicked it off that was the inspiration for writing this book. Many of the lessons you've learned in the preceding chapters come from those experiences.

The crazy part is that my company was at about a $300,000 run rate prior to our growth, meaning we hadn't even done $300K in revenue. Thus, we technically went from being about a $100K revenue company to being a million dollar revenue company in the span of a year.

All this from getting a coach, finding someone who had spent eight years getting to $3M, then compressing his eight years into a year through working with the mentor in his coaching program.

An analogy I'd use for this is traveling back in time and playing the lottery. If you were able to do that, you'd undoubtedly win because you knew all the answers already. You'd know, for example, what number or numbers would be drawn and could play those numbers.

It was no different with our mentor. We were able to take all the mentor's hindsight and pour it into our business. The hindsight from our mentor was like rocket fuel or like an injection of first-class, ultra expensive, and highly, highly illegal steroids, the sort of steroids that can turn average baseball players into household names.

Mentors, though, aren't illegal. Neither are the coaching/mastermind programs that many mentors offer. Maybe mentors and their programs should, like steroids, be banned. They can certainly give certain entrepreneurs an unfair advantage over the competition.

Still, let's not kid ourselves; this is the good kind of unfair advantage. It's completely above board and doesn't involve jamming a needle in your thigh.

No, a mentor is something you should inject into your business. My excessively long, drawn-out story has probably made that very clear. If you somehow missed the point, however, then let me put it another way. Don't worry, I'll make it quick.

Think about the greatest basketball player ever. Not Kobe. Not Lebron. They're too recent. We're talking about an older player, one who's universally acknowledged as the best. That would be Jordan. Michael Jordan.

And guess what Jordan had?

If you've spent any time listening to other coaches, or reading their literature, you probably know what I'm about to say. It's a popular argument for coaching.

I'm going to remind you that even Michael Jordan, someone who supposedly didn't need help, had a coach. It follows, then, that if Jordan had a coach, you definitely need one.

It's a catchy argument, one that makes for a good sound bite too. Hopefully, though, I've given you something more compelling with my personal example. I wanted to give you something more relevant than an example involving a legendary basketball player. That's hard to relate to as an up-and-coming entrepreneur. What you can relate to, on the other hand, is a war story like the one I've given you, something from a guy who's been in the trenches, struggling, making all kinds of dumb mistakes, and then eventually realizing the need for mentoring.

That's where I've been, and there's absolutely no need for you to end up in a similar position. If a few pages here in this book can convince you of the need to get a mentor, thereby saving yourself from years of needless struggle, then I've done my job.

We're not done, however, in this discussion of mentors. If we stopped now, you'd only have one piece of the puzzle. You'd know to get a mentor. Yet you wouldn't know how to get a mentor or how to ensure your mentor was the right one.

Let's get into those questions now.

First up is the matter of finding a mentor.

Best case scenario, you'll find your mentor organically. This was how I did it. I knew the person beforehand, saw his business, and then signed up once he began offering coaching.

If the organic approach isn't an option, then you'll need to do some research. This can be deceptively simple. In theory, you can just Google the name of your industry and the word "mentor." An example would be a real estate investor going online and doing a Google search for "real estate mentor."

This sort of search would yield hundreds of thousands of results. Somewhere in the search results could be a link to your eventual mentor's website. Still, finding that link is easier said than done. It's made all the more difficult by Ads on Google and other online marketing tactics employed by those with coaching programs.

Once more, there's the problem of how you're going to sort through it all, how you're going to separate the proverbial wheat from the chaff. How will you know which mentors are bad and which can actually benefit you and your business?

I wish there was a simple solution to this problem, some sort of silver bullet that always worked. In the absence of one, my recommendation is to take your time getting a mentor. Don't delay it, but don't rush to sign up with the first mentor you're impressed with.

Take a mentor you've found and perform some due diligence on her. Google her name and see if you can find any bad reviews. As you do this, recognize that a single bad review or two of a mentor is not an immediate turnoff.

Some mentors, for instance, have worked with so many people that one of their students is likely to have had a negative experience. Maybe that particular student didn't get a question answered by the mentor. Or maybe the student didn't get the results she wanted, yet hadn't followed the mentor's directions fully. There are plenty of other possibilities, too, any of which could have led the student to feel like the mentor had failed her and write the negative review you read.

A negative review in itself shouldn't immediately disqualify a mentor from your consideration. But ten, fifteen, or even twenty negative reviews? All from different, unaffiliated sources? That's another story.

Along with negative reviews, you can also watch a mentor's behavior online. With social media, it's possible to see how a mentor presents himself. Is he a spammer, spamming the heck out of forums? How about her Facebook and Instagram profiles? Are these profiles filled with spam and other signs that a given mentor is unethical or just plain weird? Often you'll be able to see.

Now, let's assume you find a mentor. You're able to cut through the smoke and find the one.

Your next step will be to get this person to mentor you. If the mentor you've found offers a paid coaching program, then this next step is easy. You pay the money and, voila, you get a mentor. Simple.

What about those cases when your mentor doesn't have a program that you can conveniently sign up for? In such instances, you'll need to pay careful attention to how you approach this would-be mentor, reason being that there are clear right and wrong ways to do it.

The wrong way would be to reach out to them cold with a completely selfish gimme attitude. I had this happen recently on Instagram. Someone I'd never met sent me the following message:

"Are you a real estate investor? I want to be one too, what should I do?"

My first thought: "And you are?"

I had absolutely no clue who this person was. Nor did I have any idea why I should even respond to their message.

Chances are you've gotten messages like this too, whether on social media or via email. When the messages come, what are you supposed to do? You don't know the person and they've given you no reason to respond. At the same time, you don't want to be a jerk.

So what do you do?

Nothing.

It's often easier to ignore the message; you can just delete it and move on.

Mentors are going to be of the same mind. Approach them like that guy I mentioned on Instagram, and your would-be mentor is unlikely to respond. Or, if he does respond, it'll probably be with either a helpful answer in the best case or some kind of put-down. I'd imagine this depends as well on the kind of day he's having. We're all only human, and so are even the most god-like of mentors. Approach a mentor on a bad day with a pushy request, and you might get an equally rude response.

To keep from annoying a would-be mentor, let's talk about the right way to approach her. My recommendation is to come from a place of value. Offer value rather than your own outstretched hand. Stop thinking about what she can give you and start thinking about what you can give her.

Being a giver sounds like a cliché. And maybe it is. But how else are you going to get through to a prospective mentor? We've established that you can't buy her coaching program. So apart from threatening them with a gun (illegal, by the way), you're short on options. Giving value to the mentor is thus your only shot at capturing her attention and making her want to engage with you.

Ok, but what could you possibly provide a mentor that's of value?

Great question, and I'll leave it squarely on your shoulders. You get to have fun figuring it out.

One pointer I will give you, though, is that value often comes down to time and/or skills. The mentor you want may have more money than time. Therefore, if you can give him back some of his time by offering to work for free, that could be a valuable offer. Alternatively, if you have a skill that the mentor lacks, which would make his business better, that's also something he'd see as valuable.

In this second instance, you might find a mentor who's sixty-five and clueless about social media. He wants to use social media in his business, yet when he sees #, it brings to mind thoughts of the pound sign on his landline phone.

The good news for this mentor is that you're savvy on social media. You may not have a clue about how to scale a business, as the mentor does. Nonetheless, when it comes to social media, your skill set enables you to run circles around your mentor. This forms the basis for a trade: your social media for their business skills.

That trade, by the way, may not be as explicit as I've described it. In fact, you'll often not want to explicitly ask for anything. Just continue providing the mentor with help for as long as you can, without making any requests.

Does that sound naive?

If I were in your position, I'd think so. I'd think it was downright silly to help someone who doesn't know you and never ask for anything in return. What a great way to be exploited. Running a charity for one. Letting yourself be used.

Is that a possibility?

Absolutely. But then, aren't you also using the mentor?

You're there watching the mentor and getting guidance from her, even if it's just an occasional answer to one of your questions.

It's probably a fair trade, or fairer than you might otherwise think. And if it's really so bad, you can always stop. Good mentors and coaches can be difficult to find, but that shouldn't deter you from seeking another should it become clear that you really are just being used.

*

Approaching a mentor in the way we've described — offering value — has another benefit. This goes beyond the benefit of getting the mentor's attention and not turning her off. The additional benefit is that you avoid coming off as desperate.

Think about how degrading it feels when you know your actions are perceived as desperate. No one wants, for example, to be the person at a party who's desperately seeking a ride home at the end of the night. I'm talking about an actual ride home, but you're welcome to read between the lines with that analogy.

My point is, desperation is a turnoff. It reeks like a porta-potty that hasn't been cleaned in months. No one wants to be near the smell. In fact, you might get sick just thinking about it. Same goes for desperation. It stinks, and we tend to find it sickening.

You want to avoid desperation. Avoid it at all costs, particularly when you're approaching a would-be mentor.

The best advice I can give you here is to be patient. Patience kills desperation. It's like cold water putting out the fires of desperation. Those fires may burn inside you, but with enough patience, you can douse the flames, getting to the point where a mentor won't even see the smoke.

Being patient means that you take time to write a thoughtful, well-researched email to your desired mentor. That email, your first contact with the mentor, lacks the desperation inherent in a short, rushed social media message.

Patience also means that you find a temporary solution to any money woes you may have. If you're financially desperate, bombarding a mentor with help me messages isn't the answer. You'll need to handle the money issue yourself, even if that means taking on a job and running your business part-time. Whatever you need to do on that front, do it and then approach the mentor calmly, without even a hint of desperation.

*

Let's shift now in our discussion and fill any remaining gaps in your knowledge of mentors. These next items will help to round out the experience of finding a mentor, approaching the person, and getting coaching.

I want to start by clarifying the difference between friends and mentors. This seems important since mentor-student relationships are often friendly in nature. It might seem that if you have a mentor, it's basically the same thing as having a friend, only this particular friend is providing you with guidance and support in your business.

That idea, though, is flat out wrong. A mentor is rarely if ever also a friend. The exception would be if one of your friends just so happens to be highly successful in your industry.

Barring this exception, your mentor won't be a friend. And that's usually a good thing, because your mentor needs to be further along in their journey than you and your peers. Your mentor also needs to be able to challenge you and call you out without fear of damaging a friendship.

This latter point about a mentor being critical and making you stretch is equally important when it comes to sizing up mentors. If you're beginning to work with a mentor and the person doesn't do those two things, it's time to find a new mentor.

Another sign that it's time to change mentors would be if your "mentor" commits to helping you but then doesn't do so. It's the reason I put mentor in quotes, to illustrate the difference between a "mentor" who is all talk versus an actual mentor who walks the walk too. If you end up with the former, go back to the drawing board and find someone else.

It's a red flag as well when you get a mentor who makes promises, doesn't deliver, and then wants to charge you for additional things.

Here's an example of how that could play out.

Suppose you hire a mentor and his coaching program promises to help you double your company's revenue. The program kicks off and all goes smoothly at the start. You get the same kind of insights as I did during my experience with my mentor.

Soon, however, you hit a wall in the coaching program. Your mentor has a vital piece of information to give you. Maybe it's related to hiring in order to scale your business. Maybe it's goal-setting or prospecting for new business. Regardless of what this information is, your mentor won't give it to you.

Well, that's not entirely true. He will provide you with the information. But it's going to cost you extra. This comes as a surprise, of course, since you invested money in the mentor's program with the understanding that there would not be any additional investment needed.

Assuming that was indeed the case, this mentor has misled you. Lied is actually a better way to describe it.

If you find yourself in the midst of such B.S., don't spend the extra money. Instead, spend time finding a new mentor.

Speaking of spending money, we should probably touch on that too. Crass up-sells like the one just described are clear instances of when you shouldn't spend money on a mentor. Barring these, however, I'd encourage you to be open-minded when it comes to paying for mentoring. My personal belief — even before I began mentoring people — is that value is more important than price. This means if you get enough value from a mentor, the cost of their program becomes less of a consideration.

An example would be if your business is in an industry with large transaction sizes. Real estate would be one such industry and there are plenty of others. For these industries, the difference between receiving mentoring and not receiving it can translate into millions of dollars. In this context, a $25,000 coaching program practically becomes chump change. The program's cost is infinitely less than the value you'll get from it.

In order for a coaching program to have such unbelievable value, it must fit with where you're at in your business. Make sure you don't overlook this part of the equation. Your mentor should definitely be further along in her career than you are, yet she should not be light years ahead.

That's how it might be, for instance, if you were starting your first business and being mentored by a serial entrepreneur with thirty years experience. Not to say this couldn't work, it's just that this mentor and her insights could be too high-level for you.

You'd probably be better off with a mentor who's built one successful company over the past five years. Such a mentor would have the level of success close enough to yours to seem attainable. Plus, he would probably have an easier time relating to you, the newbie, and be capable of providing relevant guidance.

While you need a mentor who can relate to you and vice-versa, your mentor does not necessarily have to be in your industry. An example of this would be with sales mentors. I've personally had mentors to help me improve my sales skills. These mentors were not specifically focused on real estate. In fact, they probably knew as much about real estate as I do about heart surgery. What my sales mentors did know, however, was how to sell. They'd passed this knowledge along to others in a variety of industries, helping their students to become top-notch salespeople. As a result, I was fine with paying these mentors to receive their guidance, despite them not having a background specific to my own field.

Just to be clear, though, this decision to seek out sales mentors came later on. It was something I pursued after I'd found success scaling my business. Until that point, I relied exclusively on mentors in my industry.

One more point about mentors: you should be cautious about having more than one. I say this with full knowledge of the "tribe of mentors" concept as popularized by the book of the same name.

Personally, I'm not opposed to the idea. But experience has taught me that having multiple mentors tends to create problems. As proof, I'd point to something I observed while running a martial arts school. I was twenty-eight at the time and had become a fourth-degree black belt.

With this ranking, I could safely be called an expert in martial arts. It was surprising, then, whenever I'd have students who attended both my school and other schools at the same time.

Did these students not trust my expertise? Did they think that what I was teaching needed to be validated by another teacher?

These questions weren't just my ego talking either. Sure, my ego wasn't OK with being two-timed, but I could look beyond that. I could be the bigger man and accept my students' need for a second opinion from another school.

Everything would have been fine if the effects of outside mentoring weren't evident. Yet they were. It was painfully obvious which of my students were attending other martial arts schools. When we'd practice techniques and do sparring, I'd observe these students feeling conflicted. They would try to fit what they were learning from me with what they were learning elsewhere.

At times, it was like watching a computer lag while trying to process information. In those moments, I could see proof that it's detrimental to have multiple mentors.

Thinking beyond martial arts, I believe that having multiple business mentors at the same time is detrimental. Doing so leads to the same problems with processing conflicting information.

One mentor, for instance, might tell you that cold calling is dead. Another mentor might give you the cold-calling scripts that enabled her to build a seven-figure business. You're left trying to make sense of cold calling. Is it really dead? Maybe. But then, this other mentor used cold calling to win big in her business. Of course, that was several years ago. So things today might really be different. Still, what if they aren't and cold calling really does work? Although...

You can drive yourself crazy with this kind of back-and-forth questioning. There's really no end to it either, since each mentor's advice can usually be defended. The only way forward is to get a single mentor and commit to following that person alone.

Later, if you want to trade your mentor for another, that's fine. This isn't like marriage, where you have to be with your mentor till death do you part. But you do need to stand by your mentor for as long as it takes to work through his program or follow his advice. If you don't and things don't turn out as you'd hoped for in your business, then the responsibility is yours alone. The mentor hasn't failed you. No, you've undermined his teaching and failed as a result.

This isn't to say that you can't have multiple mentors in different fields. I see nothing wrong with having a business mentor and also someone else who coaches you in your marriage. No conflict there. The marriage coaching won't clash with what you're hearing from your business mentor. Neither will coaching on running a marathon, meditation, or personal finance. Coaching from each of these fields and countless others can be combined without any sort of conflict. In fact, depending on where you're at, it's often a great idea.

Conflict only surfaces, as we've said, when you try to stitch together the teachings of multiple mentors in the same area. You end up with a Frankenstein-like monster that terrorizes you and kills your progress.

Moral of the story? In business at least, choose one mentor. Practice mentor monogamy, like you've been practicing book monogamy, reading only this one book.

You have been doing that, right?

You're reading just this book, and not also reading one, two, or even 10 other books simultaneously.

Provided you have, you're on track. For you've overcome two of the most formidable hurdles to success in business or even life. These hurdles are accepting outside guidance and then taking this guidance from a single source.

For the first hurdle — accepting outside guidance — think about how many people struggle with that. Imagine having a penny for every person who refused to get help, even if they knew deep down that they needed it. You'd be stupidly rich. Or at least far richer than all those people who didn't get help.

As for the second hurdle — taking guidance from a single source — that's equally challenging. We've all heard how it's important to get a second opinion or to shop around. The Internet hasn't helped things, making it easier than ever to get guidance on the same topic from millions upon millions of sources.

You can find all the information you want on the Net, from as many credible sources as your heart desires. But all of that information is worthless without execution. And execution can't happen when you're conflicted about what to do, whether because you have conflicting information or a general sense of overwhelm.

That's why I'm so adamant about the need for a single source of guidance. It's why I've encouraged you, to the point of being redundant, to take information one source at a time. Have one mentor at a time and read one book at a time.

With that latter point, you won't have long to wait. If you've been wanting to read another book, you're about to get your chance. This page and a few others are going to be the last ones I write. Meaning, this book is about to end.

*

As we do come to a close, I want to leave you with a challenge. Without knowing you personally, I can't say whether you're up to the challenge. Still, if you've made it to the end of the book — even with all my bad jokes and silly asides — then I'd say this challenge is well within your capability.

Now, here's the challenge. When you've finished reading, I challenge you to put this book down and not read another book on business or entrepreneurship for one week.

Take one week off.

In that time, get started on your business.

If you don't have a business right now, then start building it. If you already have a business, then start trying to scale it to new heights.

Spend one week taking real action. Not thinking about your business. Not researching all the different ways you could do things for the business. Not weighing all the pros and cons. Not looking for a hack or some four-hour work week trick to be more efficient.

None of that.

No, you need to Just Start.

Do it for at least a week, without running for the safety of another business book, letting that book comfort you, as you sit idly and go nowhere, as today becomes tomorrow, as tomorrow becomes someday. And as someday becomes never.

Go out there and Just Start.

When you do, you can take confidence in the fact that I've given you everything required to take action. It's all here, and you've seen that over the preceding chapters.

Moreover, you can also take heart in knowing that my challenge is only for one week.

One week is practically a joke. It's just seven days. Surely you can go that long without turning to another book. Surely, one week isn't too many days for you to spend getting started on your business either.

If it is, then I've failed you.

But if not, and you're able to go for one week, you'll find that one week is all it takes.

You won't become a millionaire with a booming business in one week. That's not what I'm saying.

My point is that one week is all it takes for you to break through, for you to get past the gravitational pull of procrastination and being a wantra-preneur.

In one week of effort — honest effort, that is — you can get a taste of what it feels like to be moving forward in your business.

This feeling can be tremendously exciting. More exciting than any book you'd read, podcast you'd listen to, or YouTube video you'd watch.

You'll never know the feeling, though, without action.

Action beginning, of course, with my challenge to you.

A challenge to put down the books.

A challenge to stop making excuses.

And a challenge to finally, finally, finally...

Just Start!

About the author

Mike Simmons began his real estate investing career in 2008, right as the market was crashing. Using the principles found in this book, he was able to build a $1 million company in less than 12 months.

Despite the apparent success, Mike remained "in the trenches" and still actively runs his company today. Along with those duties, he's also branched out into the areas of podcasting, coaching, and public speaking.

On podcasting, Mike can be heard as the host of the popular real estate investing podcast - Just Start Real Estate (**www.JustStartRealEstate.com/iTunes**). As a coach, he guides new, as well as experienced real estate investors, showing them how to start and grow their real estate investing businesses. And in public speaking, Mike can be found doing a steady stream of events each year. Past events have seen him share the stage with such household names as Gary Vaynerchuck, Ryan Serhant, Jocko Willink, Russell Brunson, Andy Frisella, Walter Bond, and Tom Ferry.

To learn more about Mike or his coaching, visit **MikeSimmons.com**. He can also be reached directly by email at **Mike@JustStartRealEstate.com**.

Made in the USA
Columbia, SC
10 August 2020